Women
WITH
Money

Also by Jean Chatzky

Women
WITH
Money

The Judgment-Free Guide to Creating

the Joyful, Less Stressed, Purposeful

(and, Yes, Rich) Life You Deserve

Jean Chatzky

GRAND CENTRAL
PUBLISHING

NEW YORK   BOSTON

Grand Central Publishing
Hachette Book Group
1290 Avenue of the Americas, New York, NY 10104
grandcentralpublishing.com
twitter.com/grandcentralpub

Originally published in hardcover and ebook by Grand Central Publishing in March 2019
First Trade Paperback Edition: March 2020

Grand Central Publishing is a division of Hachette Book Group, Inc. The Grand Central Publishing name and logo is a trademark of Hachette Book Group, Inc.

The publisher is not responsible for websites (or their content) that are not owned by the publisher.

The Hachette Speakers Bureau provides a wide range of authors for speaking events. To find out more, go to www.hachettespeakersbureau.com or call (866) 376-6591.

Print book interior design by Fearn.

Library of Congress Cataloging-in-Publication Data

Names: Chatzky, Jean Sherman, author.
Title: Women with money : the judgment-free guide to creating the joyful, less
    stressed, purposeful (and, yes, rich) life you deserve / Jean Chatzky.
Description: First Edition. | New York : Grand Central Publishing, [2019] |
    Includes index.
Identifiers: LCCN 2018037102| ISBN 9781538745380 (hardcover) | ISBN
    9781478995920 (audio download) | ISBN 9781478995913 (audio book) | ISBN
    9781538745373 (ebook)
Subjects: LCSH: Women—Finance, Personal. | Investments.
Classification: LCC HG179 .C5364 2018 | DDC 332.0240082—dc23
LC record available at https://lccn.loc.gov/2018037102

ISBN: 978-1-5387-4538-0 (hardcover), 978-1-5387-4537-3 (ebook),
    978-1-5387-4539-7 (trade paperback)

Printed in the United States of America

LSC-C

10 9 8 7 6 5 4 3 2 1

*For all the wonderful women in my life, but particularly
for Elaine, Julia, and Emily. With love.*

⌒

Contents

CONTENTS

HerMoney: An Introduction

SEPTEMBER 2017

Seven of us, all women, are at the White Dog Cafe, a restaurant in a West Philadelphia row house. It's a place more vertical than horizontal, the benefit of which is that there are more nooks and crannies than you get at airy, cavernous restaurants, which means more privacy, more space to really talk.

We are of varying ages and stages, a single woman in her 30s who just bought her first home, a married mom of two in her 40s, three divorced women in their 50s (one of whom is remarried), a two-time cancer survivor in her 60s who just left a forty-year career to embark on a new one, and a 23-year-old in her first job who tagged along with her mom. We are racially and educationally diverse; most have been to college, others through the school of life, and some have multiple or graduate degrees. At the moment, we all work, though some of us have dipped in and out of the workforce over the years to care for kids, for parents, and for ourselves. And most of us have never met before tonight.

That, as it turns out, is a good thing. Because the topic at hand is not one you might feel comfortable discussing with your closest friends. We have gathered—at my invitation, I should add—for the express purpose of talking about money. I know from past experience (this is not my first rodeo) that generating conversation about not the nuts and bolts of finances (best credit cards, mortgage rates, allowances) but about money itself is hard. People are reluctant. Even the women I know well who will talk about most things to a ready listener don't want to talk about this.

So here's what I've done: I made sure everyone I invited understood that this was the activity for the night. I made sure the wine—or beer or vodka, but let's be honest, mostly wine—was flowing. And I decided to treat it like a party game. With the help of several of my female colleagues, I came up with about thirty questions designed to spark conversation. Questions like:

- The money secret I've been keeping is _____.
- Did you have a financial wake-up call? What was it?
- I spend money because _____.
- Is it okay to hide money from your spouse (if you have one) or your partner in your underwear drawer?

I printed them out in a font large enough and clear enough that none of us would have to reach for our reading glasses, cut them into little strips of paper, put them in a Ziploc bag, and stuck them in my tote. At the gathering—which I've since dubbed a HerMoney Happy Hour—we went around the circle. Everyone, including me, pulled a question or two. And we just started talking. And talking. And talking.

Think for a moment about what it feels like to embark on a romantic relationship after a dry spell. That first touch and your nerves start to tingle. That first kiss and you're thirsty for, well, *more.*

That's kind of what it feels like to sit in a room with other women—women who are like you and not like you, kind of like you and not at all like you—and start talking about your money. It's exciting. It's empowering. It's a little bit scary. But if you start giving yourself over to the experience, the result is that you end up wanting more.

That, it turns out, is a very, very good thing.

A New Paradigm

A decade ago, I wrote a best-seller called *Make Money, Not Excuses.* Wrapped in pink, it, like other female-focused books of its time (*Prince Charming Isn't Coming, SHOO, Jimmy Choo!*) was aimed at convincing women that it was time to step up and take control of our finances.

We needed to do this because—at least for the foreseeable future— we were going to underearn men, take breaks from the workforce to care for kids and older parents that would put us behind when it came to saving for retirement, and outlive our spouses by an average of five years. That meant 90-plus percent of us would be responsible for handling our personal finances, well, *personally.* There was no getting around the fact that we would all be better off knowing how to manage our money before a crisis hit and we had to do it on the fly.

And readers loved it. It hit the *New York Times* and *Wall Street Journal* best-seller lists. Women discussed it at their book clubs. They passed it on to their friends and daughters. They kept their dog-eared copies at the ready for reference.

But things have changed. And not just a little bit. Today, women have more money—some have much more, as I'll explain in the pages to come—and though there is no denying that we are undergoing an important shift in real time in many of the workplaces across the country, marching to the drumbeat of Time's Up and #MeToo, many of us are finally also fighting for and sometimes achieving the power to go along with it.

What has also changed is what we want to do *with* our money and what we want it to do *for* us. More than ever before, we are mindful of the fact that we can, intentionally, use our financial resources to create the world we want to create—and not just for us, but for our spouses, our family and friends, and the causes we want to support.

Today, although women earners continue to lag male earners on average, there are many who have zoomed ahead. About 38 percent of

women have already become the higher earner or primary
er for their families. But that's not the only demographic
change going on. More than 50 percent of women are single—and many
will stay that way, making them de facto heads of households in their
homes. Add them in, and the primary breadwinner number soars to 60
percent.

And there's no stopping this train. For every 100 men who graduated
from college last year, 132 women graduated. Those college degrees will
drive increased earnings—increased power—for women. Already half of
all millionaires are women. Women also are poised to inherit 70 percent
of the $41 trillion in intergenerational wealth transfer expected over the
next forty years. (It's not that parents prefer their daughters to their sons,
by the way, it's that longer-living women will inherit twice—both from
their parents and from their spouses.) Over time, the wealthiest age
group in America—people age 65 and over—will continue to become
more and more and more female as the population ages.

The astonishing result: by 2028, women will control 75 percent of
discretionary spending around the world and by 2030, 66 percent of
America's wealth.

A Horse of a Different Color

Yet to take all of this additional wealth and simply plunk it into the
financial playbook that men have used for decades doesn't work because
we are different. We want to use our resources to accomplish different
things. We want to measure our progress in different ways. My friend the
best-selling author Jane Bryant Quinn once famously said, "Money isn't
pink or blue, it's green." She's right of course. But my years of research
and experience also tell me that we, as women, view money through a
different sort of lens. And that is why we need a different sort of book.

**First and foremost, for us, the life we want to create is the
target, while money is the tool that helps us achieve it. For
many men, it is the other way around.**

And there are other marked differences:

We are more concerned than men are about both economic and political issues and are willing to selectively throw money at them to create change. We are more concerned than men about the financial situations—and stability—of both our children and our grandchildren and ensuring a college education is in the cards for them. We are more concerned about leaving a legacy for our families and communities and the world. We are more concerned about using our money to help others. And we are more concerned about using our money to help ourselves—to ensure that we create a guaranteed income stream that will last as long as we do so that we can knock that one humongous worry (seriously, it's so huge that a study from Allianz revealed more people are worried about *running out of money* than they are of *dying*) off our lists.

There are major differences in the way we experience money, too: According to the American Psychological Association, women are more likely than men to already have a great deal of stress in our lives. Those stress levels are on the rise and likely to manifest in both physical and emotional symptoms. And what tops the list in terms of stressing us out? Yup. Money. And, although research has shown that—despite the annoying mansplainers who say otherwise—women are *not* more emotional overall than men, we do tend to feel negative emotions more strongly. Many of these emotions—in particular, guilt and shame, anxiousness and embarrassment—are deeply tied to our finances.

Add these things up, and it's understandable that many of us don't feel knowledgeable enough to run our financial lives with both confidence and conviction. Too many of us still prefer to sweep all things financial under the rug. Or, if we don't *prefer* to do that, then we *do* it anyway for a multitude of other reasons.

The good news is: We are ready to turn the page on all of that. According to a recent survey from Fidelity Investments, 92 percent of us want to learn more about financial planning, and 83 percent want to get more involved in our investments.

women's money goals are different

Even our perspective on risk seems to have shifted. In years past, research showed women to be more reluctant than men when it came to taking risks with our investments. That hurt us, particularly when money stashed into low-earning bank accounts could have been earning stock market returns. What we are now seeing is that the more women know about our money, the more comfortable we are taking appropriate risks. In fact, when Merrill Lynch did a study that controlled for age and lifestyle goals, the risk-taking profiles of women and men were not much different at all. What's more, 85 percent of women believe that the historical benefits of taking risk (i.e., that it's something you need to do to stay ahead of taxes and inflation and to grow your money for the long term) are here to stay.

With all that in mind, I decided to take another bite at the apple. *Women with Money: The Judgment-Free Guide to Creating the Joyful, Less Stressed, Purposeful (and, Yes, Rich) Life You Deserve* is a manual for today. It's based not just on detailed reporting with the world's top economists, psychiatrists and psychologists, behaviorists, sociologists, financial planners, accountants, money coaches, and attorneys (a life-time journalist can't change her spots), but with hundreds of real women who spoke candidly about their lives, their frustrations and fears, their hopes and dreams.

It's also deeply personal: for me. At the risk of revealing my age (okay, it's 54), I've now been covering personal finance for a quarter century. When I took my first job in this field, at *Smart Money* magazine back in 1991, I told my soon-to-be-boss I didn't want to spend my days sorting out the minutiae of 12b-1 fees.[1] He assured me that I could spend my days writing and reporting about people and their relationships with and interactions with money. And although I left that magazine long ago, I've kept his guidance close. What hasn't changed is that I still believe that life is my topic. Money is the window through which I view it.

☞ **12b-1 fees are the annual marketing or distribution fees on mutual funds. Important, yes, but a big yawn.**

But in the last twenty-five years, I have changed personally. Life does that. I've had two kids. Gotten divorced. Lost my father. Remarried (and gained two more stepchildren, and now a daughter-in-law, in the process). Watched my mother remarry (and added three stepbrothers of my own). Worried as my children struggled. Cheered as they regained their footing. Teared up as they went off to college. Let the tears flow as one graduated and then moved across the country for work. Grew concerned as my mom and stepfather started dealing with the ailments that come with age.

I've also changed professionally. When you first met me, likely on the *Today* show shortly after my firstborn (now 24) turned 1, I was an employee. *Today* was my side gig. And while I wrote books and gave the occasional speech in my spare time, I also had a job. In an office. With benefits. About a decade ago, I became one of the more than six million Americans who start a small business each year. I hired my first employee. I shopped for health insurance and started a 401(k). Today, we're still small but we're growing. We launched a website called HerMoney.com. And I've proudly watched as the young reporters I hired out of college, taught, and mentored went on to *Forbes*, the *Wall Street Journal*, and NerdWallet and grew businesses (and families) of their own.

All of that combined experience has made me more conscious of the important role that money has played—and continues to play—in my own life. But, as a woman, it's also made me more opinionated about the best ways to think about and interact with money in order to get it to produce the best results. Again, *life*—the life I want, you want, we want—is the target. There is absolutely no reason we shouldn't have it. But we need a greater understanding of and comfort with money. Because money is the tool we use to bring it about.

So, that's where this book is coming from. And this is the journey on which it's going to take you:

First, we'll take a guided tour of who we are in relation to our money. What we want from it. How our histories shape us (and how we can leave them behind if need be). Why money makes us so emotional and how it plays the role of an often uninvited third wheel in our relationships. We'll come through Part I with a greater understanding of ourselves. That will enable us to take on the more tactical, practical challenges in Parts II and III with clearer eyes.

Next up, in Part II, we'll look at managing our money to create the lives we want for ourselves. We'll talk about increasing our earning power—getting paid what we deserve, starting businesses (or side hustles), and investing for the long term (and to make the impact you want in the world). We'll take a dive into real estate. The security of having a place that is yours—and that is (eventually) paid for—is an important item on many of your financial checklists. We'll get into how to make it happen and where it fits into your other financial priorities. And we'll look at using our money in ways that bring us joy. This is not only allowed, it is encouraged.

Finally, in Part III, we look outside ourselves. (Yes, I know, we're used to focusing on others before ourselves. You'll note I flipped the script here. This is intentional.) We'll focus on using our money to raise independent, confident kids (who actually launch) and send those kids to college. We'll get into the issues involved in caring for our parents as they age. And we'll wrap it up with a discussion of leaving a legacy—the imprint you want on the world.

WHAT I SAW AT THE REVOLUTION

Throughout, you'll find yourself immersed in the stories, language, and experiences of the hundreds of women who opened up to me or one of my HerMoney colleagues by chatting with us on the phone, via e-mail, through social media, or in person with the purpose of informing this book. As we go through the chapters, you'll meet them. I've changed most of their names, and, in a few instances, some identifying detail. But I didn't change their words. I painstakingly transcribed hours of digital recordings to make sure I got them just right. Their words are their own.

As for my HerMoney Happy Hours,[2] the one I hosted in Philadelphia was just one of many such evenings (sometimes afternoons; mimosas and brunch work well, too). We've met in a home in Marin County, California, a hotel lobby in Nashville, a conference room in NYC, a restaurant outside Phoenix, and many other places. And each time, as we wound the conversation down, the reaction was largely the same: This felt different. This was special. As one woman in Marin put it, it felt *revolutionary*.

☛ **For details about how to hold your own HerMoney Happy Hour and more resources, go to: www.WomenWith MoneyBook.com.**

Which takes me back to that gathering at the White Dog in Philadelphia, where I drew the following question out of the bag:

- Who can you talk to about your money? Who can't you talk to? Why or why not?

LISA *(50s, divorced, entrepreneur): That's a really good question. Remember that movie,* Regarding Henry, *with Annette Bening. Her husband [Harrison Ford] was shot and couldn't work, and one of her friends advised her: Never tell anybody you're suffering financially. That vulnerability! I mean, I share everything— everything—really personal things with my best friends. But we've never talked about money.*

CLAUDIA *(60s, married, author): This is a really unusual conversation. I do not talk about this. It's taboo.*

MONICA *(40s, married, TV producer): You know, that's really true. I know some friends who are struggling. And maybe we talk generally about the expense of things. But we never dig in.*

JEAN: *So, do you like it? Or will you never do it again?*

CLAUDIA: *I've always felt, still do, kind of ashamed about how I've handled my money—or let my husband handle it. But I have to say it feels good to hear that I'm not alone with the things I've thought about or the things I've felt. It's* liberating.

LISA: *I agree. That's what this conversation feels like. About having power in your financial life. I deserve to have power in that.*

We all do.
Let the revolution begin.

PART I

You and Money:
An Exploration

CHAPTER 1

What Do You Want from Your Money?

Our Money, Ourselves

Once upon a time I would have said money is my currency, and then I might have said time is my currency. Now I'm at the point where I've realized it's not time that's my currency, it's contentment.

Originally, I would sacrifice my contentment in order to go to school and then work all the hours after school that I could. Later on, I started realizing time is precious and [thinking about] what my time is worth. If I wanted to do something, I would think: Well, is it worth that much money?

Now, I'm in my early 3os so [when I look at how I spend my time] is it worth me working more to earn more money I might not need compared to doing the things that I enjoy but making less?

—*Natasha, 3os, New Jersey, single, editor and publicist*

⁓

What do you want from your money?

Have you ever asked yourself that specific question? If not, you're far from alone. Most of the women interviewed for this book didn't have the sort of quick answer you'd have when responding to a query you'd been asked loads of times, like: Aisle or window? Or, how do you like your steak? They took a minute, sometimes more, to really think about it.

And the answers, when they emerged, shared an important thread. One of the things we heard over and over was that money is not an end in and of itself. It's not about amassing money—wealth—just to be rich. Instead, when we stop and take the time to think about it, we have clear, detailed answers about how we want to use it to build the lives that we envision for ourselves, our partners, our families, even the world.

But before we can get to those things, we have to conquer the four Ss.

Level Two

In 1943, a not-yet-famous psychologist named Abraham Maslow wrote a paper entitled "A Theory of Human Motivation" that was published in the journal *Psychological Review*. This was the world's first look at his Hierarchy of Needs, which we've come over time to view as a pyramid. Essentially, Maslow argued that we have to satisfy the needs at the bottom of the pyramid—the ones that are tied to our survival, like food, water, and warmth—before moving to the upper levels, where we can focus on things like finding fulfilling relationships, doing work that makes us feel valued and accomplished, and achieving our full potential.

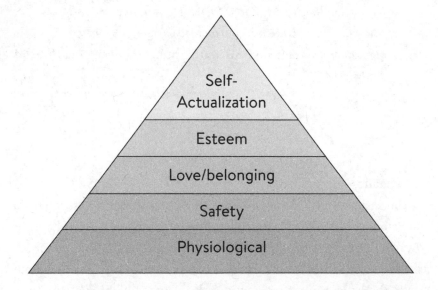

One after another, the women we interviewed told us that wh[a]t they wanted most from their money is found on Level Two. Safety. Shelter. Security. Stability.

We want that feeling of knowing that we have landed somewhere that is solid and that no other person has the ability to remove the rock from under our feet. And many of us feel we have to lock that basic need down before we can allow ourselves to want pretty much anything else from our money.

That makes sense. If you're in an environment where you feel secure and safe, comfortable and unthreatened, you're more likely to be able to move forward in your relationships, career, and overall life. If you're stressed because you fear an unpleasant surprise around the corner, not so much.

And when compared to men, we feel more insecure, more unsafe on a daily basis. This is not new. A few years ago, the Gallup Organization looked at how safe people feel walking alone at night in their own neighborhoods in 143 developed countries. Then they compared the answers of women to men. In 84 countries there were double-digit gender gaps— and high-income and upper-middle-income countries (like the United States) had some of the largest. In other words, if you're living in a nice neighborhood, with a security system (or good dead bolts), your trusty pooch by your side and still feel frightened, it is neither a) irrational nor b) unusual.

What was interesting was the ways in which this Level Two quest manifested itself. For some, like Tracey, 30s, a lawyer in New York, it means a house, plain and simple. "We purchased our house before I got pregnant," she says. "I wanted that stability." Ariel, a 36-year-old antiques store owner from New Jersey, concurs. "Success is my home and what my home represents," she says. "Money is the tool to get there."

I can totally relate. When I got separated and then divorced, about a dozen years ago, I was laser focused on buying a house—and making it a place my kids would be comfortable and I could curl up and decompress when they were with their dad. I wanted cozy, with nooks to read and watch TV. I wanted warmth. Never mind that real estate prices were so high that even if I sold today, I wouldn't get what I paid. (I went to contract in May 2005. The bubble popped the next year.) Renting would have made considerably more sense, and yet I wouldn't even think about it. It had to be mine so that no one could take it away from me. In fact, when I remarried a few years later, I refused to let my new husband buy in. For me, it was enough to *buy* the house. For other women, the need runs deeper. They want to *own* it outright. Christine, 30s, a business coach from Kentucky, says one of her "big goals" is to pay off her mortgage, noting, "I think there's something psychological about having that."

SAFETY GIRLS

The desire for safety popped up in other ways as well (making me think of when Julia Roberts presented a panoply of condoms to Richard Gere in *Pretty Woman*, telling him matter-of-factly, "I'm a safety girl").

We heard a lot about safe cars. "My husband feels like there's [a set of expectations] that this is where the successful people in our community live, this is the kind of car they drive. He gets caught up in that," says Lisa, 50s, who runs a health and wellness business in Wisconsin. "I'm more concerned about safety features as I'm carting my kids around." Riki, 40s, from Arizona, agrees. "My feeling is that it's okay that I'm not driving a Ferrari, but I need at least a very safe car and a car that's reasonably new," she says, "which is why I lease all the time." (Again, just for the record, I'm on the same page as both. I drive a Volvo—wait for it—station wagon.)

But there is also a large cadre of women for whom safety is even more, well, literal.

SAFETY = SAVINGS

The Merriam-Webster dictionary, editions of which have been published since 1828 (who knew!) has a veritable laundry list of meanings for the word *save* when used as a verb. Among them:

- To deliver from sin
- To rescue or deliver from danger or harm

- To preserve or guard from injury, destruction, or loss
- To put aside as a store or reserve

Forgetting the first (it was at the very top of their list, so I had to include it), for many women the safety and security that can come from money is best found in actual savings. As in money. In. The. Bank. Kathleen, 40s, a single mom from New York, explains:

> *It's a huge feeling of safety for me to have money saved. In fact, I sold my apartment in Brooklyn before I adopted my son and ended up in the suburbs, and now I rent. And what I like about that is I feel strongly about hanging on to my money. I know it's [not as smart as investing it would be] but I feel pretty uneasy at this point about money, and one thing that makes me feel a little bit better is seeing a balance in various—so called—safe places right now.*

Heather, 50s, a literary agent in New York, has experienced a similar desire to hoard cash at points in her life where she was about to take on more risk in her career. "The first time I quit a big job, I *needed* some $800,000 in the bank from a home sale to feel confident enough to take that leap." Interestingly, as she became more certain of her ability to keep earning, the amount she needed in the cash stash lessened significantly. The second time she quit a big-paying job, she had an $80,000 cushion—and when she eventually quit corporate life entirely to launch her own firm, a tenth of that. "I think once you learn that you can catch yourself when you're leaping and flying, that net doesn't need to be so large," she says. "Instead, you realize you are the net."

Beyond Savings: Freedom

Once we've achieved a certain level of safety, or satisfied any other more primal needs, *then* what is it we want from our money?

Actually, that's the wrong question. There are as many answers to what is it *we* want from our money as there are colors on the Pantone wheel. The right question is what do *you* want from your money, which is another way of asking what do *you* want from your life.

Going through the process of figuring this out—which we are going to do together in a moment—is likely to require a pencil and some paper. You'll want a quiet space. It's not a one-and-done kind of thing, but rather something you'll start, put down, go back to, and pick up again. And it will, as many women noted, change as you age and change yourself. That's to be expected and perfectly fine. You'll revisit and tweak and forge ahead.

The point is that for all but the very, very wealthiest people on the planet, money is a limited resource. We will be happiest about how we use our resources if we can line them up with the things that line up most closely with our values. Things, importantly, can be both tangible and intangible. Tangible ones—like the houses or the safe cars or the clothes that make us feel confident and polished, or the Labrador retriever who makes every day better by greeting us at the door—are easy to get a grip on because we can envision them. Intangibles are harder to express because they're more difficult to see—but they tend to come out in words like *freedom, flexibility,* and *time.* For example:

- Freedom to leave a bad relationship. *Having money gave me the peace of mind to know that being unhappy in a marriage didn't mean I needed to stay in it because I didn't have financial security. That was a big thing for me. I'm really lucky because I know there are women who couldn't do what I did.* (Zoe, 40s, divorced, nonprofit director, New York)

- Freedom to leave work you don't love. *I worked, pretty much all my life, and never really loved it. So the fact that I don't have to work anymore and I can do whatever I want is great.* (Carol, 60s, married, retired, North Carolina)

- Freedom to give back. *I'd love to spend the second half of my life volunteering. We're on the right track now, but we've still got a ways to go.* (Jenn, 30s, married, commercial banker, Tennessee)

- Freedom from financial risk. *When I have enough money that I don't have to risk it in the market any longer and I'm able to live off that . . . I'll know I've achieved financial security.* (Gina, 30s, married, CEO, Michigan)

- Freedom from asking permission. *[I'd like] to be able to do what I, myself, want to do . . . have a roof over my head, pay my bills, drive to work, communicate with my family, spend quality time with my friends . . . without having to be concerned about [anybody else]. If I think it's reasonable to do what I want to do with the money, I want to be able to do it.* (Natasha, 30s, single, editor and publicist, New Jersey)

- Freedom to stop thinking about money at all. *Real success for me would be to not care about money anymore—to feel that we have enough of it that I don't need to worry about it. But the more money I make, the more I think that's not really an attainable goal.* (Kristin, 30s, engaged, social media manager, Vermont)

The Intangible Wild Card: Time

There's one other big variable in this equation: time. More specifically, your time.

It was a man, sadly, who first said that "time is money." I had hoped it was one of those brilliant queens that Judi Dench plays in the movies. It was Benjamin Franklin. And the full passage reads like this:

> *Remember that Time is Money. He that can earn Ten Shillings a Day by his Labour, and goes abroad, or sits idle one half of that Day, tho' he spends but Sixpence during his Diversion or Idleness, ought not to reckon That the only Expence; he has really spent or rather thrown away Five Shillings besides.*

Franklin had the math right, but the sentiment wrong—particularly for our chockablock days. Our challenge is figuring out not just when time is money, but when money can be time. When does it make sense to use our money to free up our time for endeavors that are more meaningful or valuable than working? When can money be used to remove some of the stress associated with doing a particularly difficult or unwelcome task ourselves? Think about small things like ordering in when you just don't want to cook, hiring a car to take you to the airport because parking is a nightmare, getting a blowout because…well, just because.

Then, think of the bigger ones. Money can buy you the time to spend with a friend you haven't seen in forever (or one you see all the time but can't get enough of). It can buy you time to spend with a parent who's not doing well, time to work an hour less each day so you can explore a new pastime, to stay home part- or full-time with a child. It bought Christin, 30s, a new mom in Washington State, a year at home with her newborn son. "I know that I am very fortunate and many people don't get this luxury," she says. "But I am grateful for every day I have with him."

The goal is to think about it almost analytically—to figure out at what points in your life applying the money-to-time-conversion math makes sense for you as Gina, the 30-something CEO from Michigan, explains:

> I run my own company. So the more I work, typically the more I will earn. [Sometimes,] I will overwork to make sure I'm saving at a higher rate so I don't have that additional stress and concern. [Other times, I make the decision to trade] business time for personal time. I certainly do everything within my control not to spend those extra evenings at the office that I could be home with my family. And last year before my oldest daughter went off to college, I made the professional decision to take every Friday off that summer to spend as much quality time as I could with all three of my girls together while they were all still at home.

WANTS VS. NEEDS FOR GROWN-UPS

So, let's figure it out. What do you want your money to do for you?

When we're teaching financial literacy to children, one of the first issues is to get them to separate needs from wants. A warm coat? Need. A jersey with the logo of your favorite team? Want. Lunch? Need. Lunch at the new sushi place on the corner? Want.

They get it almost immediately. But then they grow up and it turns out we've been feeding them a bunch of baloney (sometimes literally). Behavioral economist Sarah Newcomb explains that the strict dividing line approach has several problems. First, there are needs and then there is a whole array of approaches to meeting that need. You need transportation. Does that mean you need a car? A luxury car? Perhaps not, when transportation could be a bus. A bike. Uber.

The second—and perhaps bigger issue for women—is that when we tell ourselves that anything not essential to our basic survival is unnecessary, we're ignoring a whole, vast category of needs: our emotional ones.

For Newcomb herself, beauty is a need. "It is incredibly important in my life," she says. "I feel comforted by it. I get a lot of enjoyment from beauty. And so, for me, beautiful clothing and having a home that is beautiful are really deep needs." Your emotional needs may be different. Comfort. Luxury. Excitement. The key is accepting that a) they are needs, b) they are not irrational, and c) you're going to be unhappy if you don't find ways to meet them. Then you can go about doing exactly that with the resources you have. They don't have to be all that pricey, either. Newcomb has learned that a bubble bath enjoyed while sipping a nice glass of scotch and listening to some "slow jams" can bring on a feeling of beauty and luxury that is deeply satisfying and personal to her.

That's important. Because the third issue is that trying to ignore your needs simply doesn't work. You know this if you've ever been hangry. You go through your day without stopping to eat, and for a while it doesn't matter. Then your stomach starts sending signals to your brain that it's waiting. Send a little something my way, it asks you. Doesn't have to be much, a yogurt maybe, or a Kind bar. But you're on a roll and you ignore it. And a little while later, you're over the precipice, so cranky you're going to eat the last eight Mallomars—dammit. Never mind the fact that you know your kids will want one before bed. Never mind knowing that no one ever wants to think about the fact that they just downed eight Mallomars. Our emotional needs are just like the feelings of being hangry. They get louder and more insistent if we try to ignore them.

And the fourth, and final, issue is that we are surrounded by needs that are not our own, but that others—friends, relatives, advertisers—want us to embrace as our own. These are the *should*s. Anytime you catch yourself thinking of doing something or buying something because it is expected of you or because you're trying to keep up—with trends or with other people—you are likely in should territory. Shoulds should be avoided at all times.

Syncing Our Values with Our Spending

It doesn't matter if we're talking about a little bit of money or a lot; if we can get to the point where we are lining up our values with our spending, we are going to feel better about how we are using our resources. We are going to feel as if we're getting more value from our money.

Here are two exercises to help you do this. The first looks backward. The second looks ahead.

EXERCISE 1
Look Backward

For the next month, keep a log of everything you spend. I don't care if you charge it, pay cash, or use Venmo; write it down. Then, at the end of

---

each week, go back and make a note of how you feel—in hindsight—about the money that you spent. What you'll start to notice is that you feel really great about some expenditures and not so great about others. Those not-so-great ones are signs that you could be using your money better. If you're resentful that you're spending money on a gym because you don't like that particular gym—perhaps the smell of the locker room gives you middle-school flashbacks—ask yourself: How else could I use these resources to service the same need for staying in shape? New running shoes? A class a week at a chic spinning studio?

∼

EXERCISE 2
Look Ahead

One of the most popular episodes of my *Her-Money* podcast was an interview with Samantha Ettus, author of *The Pie Life: A Guilt-Free Recipe for Success and Satisfaction*. Ettus's theory is that there are seven pieces in each of our life pies—family, work, relationship, hobbies, health, friends, and community/religion—and that we have to be fulfilled in each of them to be satisfied in our lives overall. The amount of time and energy that we devote to each piece of the pie changes as our lives shift and change through the years. Hobbies, for example, might take a backseat when we're focusing on building our work lives or raising our kids, but ride shotgun as we retire and look for something meaningful to do with our free hours.

But, she notes, even if you're not devoting much time at all to a particular area right now, it's important to represent it with a sliver of pie so that you can revisit it later. It's time to fill out your own pie plate. Just ballpark it and scratch in some percentages. How much time are you spending on:

_____ *Family*
_____ *Work*
_____ *Relationship*
_____ *Friends*
_____ *Health*
_____ *Community/Religion*
_____ *Hobbies*

Now step back and ask, how does that look to you? Is it about right? Would you rather be spending more time/energy/resources on family and less on work? How much? Perhaps you can figure out a way to turn your five-day workweeks into four-day ones to give you an extra chunk of time at home. Or, if you're in the midst of training for a big physical challenge, it's likely that health is eating up a lot of your pie right now. What happens when the race/event is over? Maybe you could start taking a weekly hike with a friend you've been missing in those hours you'll no longer be training. You'll still get the endorphins from the physical activity, plus you'll expand your friends slice by spending more time with her.

Once you've got a sense of where your values lie, you can move toward using your financial resources to get you there. It's not an overnight transformation, but these suggestions may help.

～

Suggestion 1: Give up the ghost (of guilt).

I'm Jewish, so believe me when I say I get guilt. I not only get it, I suffer from it and have a hard time escaping it—even when I try. But try we should. Guilt takes a toll on our productivity, creativity, efficiency, and concentration. It makes it difficult to enjoy whatever it is we're doing. And guilty feelings, according to psychologist Guy Winch, take up about five hours per week.

What exactly is guilt? In the legal sense, it involves having committed a crime. In the emotional one, it's feeling you've failed to do something you were supposed to do. A lot of guilt comes from our inner voices—including the feeling that we're doing better in our lives (or the world) than we deserve. But other people can lay on the guilt in order to get us to do things their way. As it relates to our money, that can mean using our resources (or time) to do things they want us to do—buy things, contribute to their charities, attend to their priorities—rather than things we want to do.

From within or without, it's crucial to recognize that whether we actually give in to that guilt is a choice. We can choose to not buy in—to decide that *our* feelings of how we should use *our* time and *our* resources are in fact more valid than those of anyone else. If you are a chronic sufferer, that's easier said than done. So how do you eliminate it? On my podcast, Ettus offered one method that has been working for me. "The thing to realize is that when you're feeling guilty, literally no one is winning, and someone—and I would argue more than one person—is losing," she said. "You're losing because it affects your stress and your health, and that, of course, impacts your kids and your partner and your friends and anyone around you." Her solution is to try to be more present everywhere you are.

It works. "If you're giving 110 percent at the office, it's much easier to go home and shut that off. If you're with your kids at night and you're turning off the phone and spending two hours literally listening to them, engaging with them, it's worth more than eight hours of distracted parenting," Ettus explains. I concur. Being there with the kids, or your partner, is also the antidote to spending money you don't particularly want to spend to compensate for the fact that you're not around.

Suggestion 2: Cop to your own excuses.

As I mentioned in the introduction, I wrote a whole book about these a decade ago. *Make Money, Not Excuses* detailed how the stories we tell ourselves get in the way of plowing ahead and taking hold of our financial lives. The book lined up and then knocked down the most common money excuses at the time.

- I don't know where to begin…
- I'm not good with math (numbers)…
- I'm too disorganized to deal with my money…
- I don't have any time…
- But my husband does that…
- I have nothing to wear…

In order to fight your own excuses, you have to first recognize that you're making them. So, start listening to yourself. And then pick one excuse that you want to focus on at a time and approach it like you'd approach any other goal. Break it into manageable pieces. Take one step at a time. Once you've taken each step, allow yourself to recognize and feel good about the fact that you've made progress. Then move on to the next.

If you're telling yourself you don't have time for money, try freeing up fifteen minutes every day to do something financial: Read the business section of the paper. Start organizing your accounts so they make sense. Start researching financial advisors.

Suggestion 3: Accept that you deserve it.

Another thing that may be standing in your way is your own inability to be giving to yourself. In order to get what you want from your money, you have to accept that you deserve this money—in other words, give yourself permission to have it and enjoy it.

There have been umpteen studies about why women still earn just (about) four-fifths of a dollar for every dollar a man earns. This is true even when you look at a playing field that should ostensibly be level. A 2016 study published in *JAMA Internal Medicine* looked at the salaries of male and female doctors. It methodically compared apples to apples—looking at docs with the same specialties, years of experience, localities—and still found women earning an average of $20,000 less a year. When asked why, the study's lead author told *Time* magazine that it's because women a) don't negotiate and b) don't go out and get offers from other employers so that they can go back to their current one with evidence that they should be paid more.

Why don't we? In part, it's because we understand (and again research backs this up) that advocating aggressively for ourselves at work comes at a high social cost. In the eyes of other people, our likability goes down. (Just ask Hillary Clinton. When she was advocating for the country as secretary of state, her polling numbers were through the roof. When she was advocating for herself as candidate for president, not so much.)

But we may also not be sure that we deserve it—that we're worth it. Jennifer, 30s, a health insurance executive with a young child, was living in California when she and her husband decided they wanted to move back home to New Jersey. Jennifer approached the CEO of her company about it and he said fine—but that he was taking $20,000 off her annual salary because of what her move would cost him. "I was grateful to keep my job and so I went along with it, even though I thought it was ridiculous," she said. But once the move was under her belt, she took a look at her workload and realized just how much it had increased. And she went back to that CEO and pointed out that he had docked her twenty grand while giving her double the work. "It became a conversation," she said.

Heather, the New York literary agent, had a similar experience a little over a decade ago. At the time, she was not an agent, but a book editor—a stellar one, mind you, who routinely had two or three books on the *New York Times* best-seller lists. Her two children were 1 and 5, and she wanted to work from home on Fridays. The female head of her department would only allow it with a four-day workweek and a 20 percent reduction in salary. Heather took the deal with the understanding that the four-day week was supposed to grant her a similar reduction in work. "Needless to say, that didn't work," she shares. "The resentment I felt at the cut when I was their top producer and trying to now shove what was always a seven-day workload into four to make up for it led me straight back to the five-day workweek at my former pay after a few months."

Now, a decade and a half later, Heather says, she would have told them where they could stick their four-day week. "There's no way I would undervalue myself in that way."

The key to dealing with this, says business strategist Leisa Peterson, is learning to question your assumptions of what's right, what's allowed, and what's outside of that. If something falls outside the lines and it's standing in your way of living your life to the fullest, it's time to go back and explore why. Why are you not allowing yourself to have these things—or *do* these things—even though, from a strictly financial purview, they are absolutely possible right now? And what would happen if you changed that?

What Have We Learned

- *When considering what we want from our money, the need for safety and security is primal.*

- *Our emotional needs should not be discounted or dismissed.*

- *We'll be most satisfied if we use our money to accomplish things that line up with what we value most—and these values are individual.*

Where Do We Go from Here

Why are your money wants, needs, values, and fears different from those of other women? They weren't raised in your town, in your house, or with your parents and your experiences. Your money story colors the way you walk through life. It's the most fascinating one you've never read.

CHAPTER 2

Your Money Story
(and How It Affects You to This Day)

Christine's Money Story

I learned different things from each of my parents. My mom is a CPA by training. She was a stay-at-home mom but very conscientious. And she paid all the bills. I learned from her that we spend money on things that are practical. But there's not enough for the big dreams. My dad worked very hard and made good money, but would find ways to sneak me a $20 here and there. He'd say: Don't tell your mom. He had more of a playful attitude toward money that was in contrast to my mom. [The result] is that I think my money story is that there's never enough so I'm not enough.

∼

YES, YOU HAVE A MONEY STORY

When you consider the powerful influences over your financial life—if you've ever done that before now—maybe you tick off the books you read, television shows you watched, college you attended, neighborhood you grew up in. Those are all real and potentially made an impact on you. But the most powerful force in your financial life *to this day* is quite possibly something you've never really considered, something about which you're not really quite aware.

Some experts call it your money story. Others call it your money script. Essentially, it's the impact your childhood had on your core memories of money.

But your money story does not comprise the things your parents or the people who raised you tried to teach you. Your money story is not the save/spend/give jars your well-intentioned parents lined up on your dresser when you were seven and they decided to teach you fiscal responsibility. It's not the first trip to the bank, where you met the teller and got a Dum Dum lollipop (butterscotch, please). It's not even the grandparent who introduced you to the stock market by suggesting that you follow the ups and downs of Walmart together. Those are lessons. They are memories. They are tales you might tell—and even attempt to repeat—with your own kids.

Your money story starts earlier, around age 3 or 4. It crept into you as you watched, listened, absorbed. Every day. It was the fact that there was, or wasn't, tension in the air on payday, at holidays, at bonus time. In the looks your parents shot each other when one wasn't pleased with the way the other handled something. In the shingles that were painted the minute they started to show signs of wear, or the ones that chipped away until neighbors started to whisper. A child's first view of how something is handled typically becomes, in their minds, the way something *should* be handled. (Although sometimes it flips and becomes the way something *should not* be handled, but we'll get to that in a moment.)

Think about your view of romantic relationships, suggests Ryan McPherson, a financial planner. Whatever it is has absolutely everything to do with the type of marriage or relationship you experienced your parents having when you were a young child. It's the same with money. "When you're young, you think your parents know everything, so the way they handle or mishandle money is tremendously impactful on how you believe money should be handled," he says. But it's not just their handling of it, it's how *you* experience their handling of it.

But your story has as much—if not more—to do with you than it does with the people who raised you. Children believe the universe revolves around them and that everything happens because of something they did or thought or said. Think about all those children of divorce who were sure that it happened because they misbehaved. The result is that two children who grew up in the same environment can wind up with wildly different scripts.

Financial advisor Ellen Rogin recalls giving a workshop where a mother attended with two daughters. Rogin asked the participants to share what their earliest memories with money were, and one daughter said: "My mom always spent money we didn't have and I knew that and now I'm a really good saver." But the other followed up with: "We never worried about money then, so I don't worry about it now." Same family. Different take.

But no matter what your environment was like, chances are pretty good that your parents didn't talk much about money on a regular basis. That made what you witnessed (or thought you witnessed) your truth even if it wasn't quite your reality.

And for peeks at other financial lives to give you perspective? There likely weren't many—if there were any at all. As Brad Klontz, a financial therapist,[3] points out: "You can go to a friend's house and watch how their parents interact as a couple. But you really can't get a sense of how these people are managing money or what their relationship with money is like." Why? Because chances are they weren't talking about it in front of their own kids—so they certainly weren't going to put it on display in front of you. That made it particularly hard to fact-check your beliefs in real time.

☞ These financial therapists I cite? There are many, and some have been helpful resources of mine for years. You'll find the ones we talked to listed in Sources and Resources in case you decide you want to read more of their work or even try to climb on their couches.

What did you do with this all-important story once you'd built it? You locked it away in a place deep inside you and built your entire relationship with money around it—without giving it the opportunity to be questioned, or challenged, or explored. It never saw the light of day. You may not even have been aware of it.

Until now.

Virginia's Money Story

When I was 9 we moved to a pretty ritzy suburb. In my old neighborhood, everybody around me was middle or working class. When we moved, the kids had different brands of things. I had the wrong sneakers. The wrong backpack. It took me a while before I understood what I was really supposed to want.

I think that middle-school stuff gave me a template for my feelings [today]. If I have a big work meeting, I'm going to go out and buy a new outfit probably. There's that sense of wanting to feel that I'm in a place in my life financially where I can throw money at the problem and solve it that way.

~

Let's Dig Deeper

Most people—if they've considered their money story at all—have just scratched the surface. They've thought back enough to run an if-then scenario that goes something like:

My father was very controlling about money.

Therefore, I'm going to be a penny-pincher for the rest of my life.

It's a start. But it's time to go deeper. The first thing to understand is that children learn in one of four ways.

1. Imitation. Children see something happening and they do it, too. From your perch in the shopping cart, you watched your mother check to see which brand of cereal was on sale each week. You might find yourself doing the same, just like you smell the cantaloupes in the exact way she did. Classic peekaboo behavior.

2. Listening. They hear words and believe those words are in fact true. Sometimes, those words represent truths like "the

stove is hot." But other times, they represent beliefs, like "no one ever got rich without cheating." Grow up believing that, and it's understandable if you feel guilt and trepidation about asking for a raise.

3. Specific experiences. There was an incident at school or at home. Perhaps you remember a huge argument every month at bill-paying time. You may grow up feeling that you don't want to deal with money because money creates arguments.

4. Absorption. Children tend to absorb the emotions of their parents. So, maybe there was no incident or argument, but rather a low-lying current of stress or resentment. Or maybe it was the complete opposite: there was a feeling of safety or joy. Either way, you took it in and processed it and now it's a part of you.

I tell you this because, as we go through the series of questions that come next, I want you to think about not just what you were told—but what you heard, saw, thought, and felt.

I want you to be *introspective*.

Introspective (and I know this because I don't particularly like to look inward—as the numerous therapists I've quit can attest) is hard. Introspective can be uncomfortable. Introspective makes you want to get up from the computer (or the book) and clean out the freezer or run to the dry cleaner or check your child's math homework (for the second time). Try to go with it instead.

A couple of directions about this exercise: First, do it alone. If you have a partner, ask that person to do it as well. Later, you can sit down and talk about your answers together. Second, although you may want to take time to jot down your answers (the margins are a fine place for this, or if you're reading an ebook or listening, grab a pen and paper), you also want to go through this pretty quickly the first time. We'll go back through them when you're done, but on the first pass the whole idea is not to censor yourself. Whatever bubbles to the top is very likely the truth.

EXERCISE 3

THE MONEY QUESTIONS

What was the feeling about money like in the home where you grew up?

_____

_____

_____

What was the feeling like about spending money?

_____

_____

_____

What was the feeling like about saving money?

_____

_____

_____

What was the feeling like about giving money away?

_____

_____

_____

What's your earliest money memory?

_____

_____

_____

What messages did your mother pass down to you about money? (Note: messages are different than lessons like how to balance a checkbook.)

_____
_____
_____

What messages did your father pass down to you about money?

_____
_____
_____

Do you remember hearing your parents talk about (or fight about) money?

_____
_____
_____

Growing up, did you have more than/less than/about the same as your peers?

_____
_____
_____

RECOGNIZING YOUR STORY IN YOUR LIFE TODAY

Done? Excellent.

Now we're going to go through it again—a little more slowly. Look at your answer to each individual question and then pause to ask these three follow-ups:

- How is this affecting me in my life today?
- How is this helping me?
- How is this hurting me?

Perhaps the answer to the first question—*What was the feeling about money like in the home where you grew up?*—was tension. Money caused tension. When you think back, that's the feeling you get.

So, now you take the three follow-ups:

How is this affecting me in my life today? Maybe you still feel the tension. Whenever you're faced with any substantial money decision—whether it's figuring out how much is reasonable to spend on renovating the bathroom or whether to take the job you don't really want but that pays more than the one that makes you happy, you get tied up in knots. You can feel it in your gut. It makes it difficult to move forward.

How is this helping me? Perhaps the fact that money causes you to shut down has stopped you from making some unfortunate decisions. Maybe you were willing to let your employer default you into a mix of investments for your 401(k) that were appropriate for your age, rather than choosing them yourself—and that turned out for the better.

How is this hurting me? Let's go back to that job decision for a moment. If you recalled—or just had a feeling—from childhood that the tension in your home tailed off in years when your parents were more flush, then perhaps you opted for the position that paid more, even though it didn't make you quite as happy. Or, maybe the ramifications are simpler and more straightforward. Perhaps the tension means it just takes you an insanely long time to shop for anything—because you have trouble making decisions. That's an issue to be dealt with as well.

And this is just one example of how it might play out when you follow the bread crumbs. Here's another—from real life.

Alyssa's Money Story

The narrative in our family was poverty. My dad is a financial planner—that's his job. But he raised us with values of poverty. Whenever we were going to play a game of Ms. Pac-Man, he'd say, "Well, you might as well just throw that money in a ditch." I thought we were on the verge of food stamps.

But there was another side to it. One night we were in the Dairy Queen and everyone kept coming up to him and talking to him. And it turned out, he owned the Dairy Queen, and I had no idea. Because we spent the weekend going to garage sales. And so now, I'm still always thinking about what things cost. And even though we are doing just fine, I always feel broke.

If this was your story, the first time through you would likely have focused on the childhood messages that spending money was wasteful and thoughtless. And perhaps that you didn't have enough. The ownership of the Dairy Queen—and the fact that it was a secret from the family or at least the children—sends a conflicting message: Having money is bad, shameful, undesirable. You shouldn't talk about it and you shouldn't show it off. And the manifestations in Alyssa's adult life are clear: Even though she has plenty of money, she still doubts every purchase, wondering whether this, too, is the equivalent of throwing money in a ditch.

THE LINES AREN'T ALWAYS CLEARLY DRAWN

Financial therapists and some financial planners who do psychological assessments spend their days going through exercises just like this with their patients and clients—and they attest that sometimes the lines between yesterday's messages and today's feelings and behaviors are precisely this clear.

The analysis gets a little tougher, though, when our reaction isn't to repeat our money stories, but to do the opposite. Instead of trying to replicate what happened in our childhoods, we reject it and go in the other direction. Sometimes we mirror what we *didn't* see. For example, perhaps you grew up in a family where your primary earning parent was always in and out of work. You were never sure where the next job was going to come from, but in the end your parent always landed on his feet. What you took from this depends on how you experienced the instability. For some, the upshot is: Life is really crazy, but the future will take care of itself. For others: Life is really crazy, and I never want to go through that again.

Melissa, 46, a divorced medical device sales rep from Philly, is a prime example of someone trying to course correct for her childhood. Her parents were so bad with money that they lost their family farm to foreclosure.

Melissa's Money Story

Way back in the day before caller ID and answering machines, I would always have to answer the phone at night and talk to the bill collectors. There was a woman named Mrs. Black, and she would always call and ask for my parents, and even though they were sitting there, I'd have to say that they weren't there. That's my memory, having to be the person in the family that answered the phone because there were so many bill collectors calling, and having to lie for my parents.

What scares me now is having money—I don't make a huge amount based on East Coast standards, but I make a huge amount based on the standards in Wisconsin, where I grew up. I like the benefits of having it in my life, but I don't want it to define me with people who aren't in the same position as me. I purchased a convertible two years ago, a silver 370Z with a black top. It's a midlife-crisis car. I paid cash for a ridiculous

car that I love but I'm embarrassed to drive because I've been
careful of not showing that I have money.

∽

Hey, There's Another Person in My Bed

Getting a grip on your own money script is complicated enough. You double that when you add a partner or a spouse to the equation. We're often drawn to people because they have very different money scripts than we do. If you're anxious about money, you may be really attracted to someone who seems to really enjoy life. You look at that person who is really enjoying life—it looks like it feels fantastic—and you think: I want to be a part of that. On the flip side, if you're somebody who's a little more care-free, then you might find yourself drawn to a person who seems stable and thoughtful and planned out around money. There can be some real beauty in that we can be attracted to someone who, in effect, balances us out.

This, by the way, may not have been a choice you made consciously. For all the articles on how couples *should* discuss finances (from the tactical *What's your credit score?* to the ephemeral *How do you feel about saving versus spending?*) when they're dating, we know most do not. But there's a lot you can tell about a person's financial peccadilloes just by being around them, and as a result we may find ourselves with someone whose perspective is, if not diametrically opposed, then at least somewhat opposed, to ours. The result is often tension.

As Riki, 40s, from Arizona, explains, in her husband's prior marriage he lived in a 6,000-square-foot home with a giant yard complete with a swimming pool (and a slide!). She lived in a one-bedroom apartment. Today, they're in a 3,000-square-foot home in a gated community. To her, it's luxurious. To him, embarrassing. She says:

He won't throw dinner parties. He will not have friends over
because he's so humiliated by this backyard. But all these

people are our friends and they've had us over at their houses.
And they've had us to their kids' Christmas plays. I say to him:
"You must be kidding."

Tension like that can be dangerous. Research from Jeffrey Dew at Utah State University revealed that the more frequently couples fight about money, the more likely they are to divorce. And as money is the thing couples fight about *most* (more than household chores, togetherness, sex, snoring, and what's for dinner, according to a 2014 *Money* magazine survey of married couples with $50,000-plus household incomes), that's a problem.

What tends to happen is that partners expend a lot of time and energy trying to convince the other person that they're right. We want our partners to adopt our deeply held beliefs. And, in our efforts to do that, we start to exaggerate our own ways of thinking. It's a little like politics.

A moderate Democrat falls for a moderate Republican. She's charmed by his views on fiscal restraint and relieved that he sides with her on social issues. He thinks it's adorable that she doesn't mind paying more for social programs, and admires her passion. Then Congress begins debating a new tax bill, or the Supreme Court takes up an abortion case. Every night at dinner he tries to convince her that his way of thinking is the right way of thinking. Every morning over toothbrushing she tries to convince him that he should—in his heart—really feel her way. They go to work grumpy and to sleep resentful, wondering: *Will there be sex tonight? Tomorrow? Ever again?*

This is no way to live. We'll dive deeper into these issues in Chapter 4, Your Money and Your Relationships. But for now, understand that finding someone whose money experience is the perfect lock to your key just doesn't happen. Everyone's history and therefore everyone's money story is unique. Try to adopt the attitude that it's a good thing. "It's almost like diversifying a portfolio," says financial therapist Amanda Clayman. "In the portfolio of what you each bring to this family system, [you're building] a broader set of combined skills." And, like happy marriages of political opposites, once you understand each other's beliefs—and how your partner is likely to interpret, and react to, the events of the day—you can moderate your own responses. As Democratic political strategist James Carville—perhaps as famous for his more-than-two-decade marriage to Republican political strategist Mary Matalin as he is for coining the phrase "It's the economy, stupid"—once wrote, "I'd rather stay happily married than pick a fight with my wife over politics."

You Can Change Your Destiny

The other thing to understand is that your childhood experience does not dictate your financial destiny. Once you know what your story is—and have gained some insight into how it's impacting your day-to-day life, then you can start to challenge it. You can decide that you no longer want to live the same way, with the same feelings. Which isn't to say it's as easy as flipping a switch.

You can't cancel old programming. "And you can't just wish this part of you away," says Clayman. "You can't undo it. And even knowing about it doesn't make it magically disappear." What you want to do instead is reprogram in a positive way. To do this, you'll need a good grip on your rationale. Why do you want more money? Why do you want to be wealthy? Why do you want to invest? Why do you want to save? What do you want to avoid? Getting a handle on your motivation will help you figure out if you're pursuing the right life for you. Or, as they say again and again on *The Bachelorette*, are you doing this for the #rightreasons? Then you can go about changing your ways deliberately.

For example, if you were raised to believe—like Alyssa, the Dairy Queen daughter—that spending money is bad or wasteful and as a result you have trouble spending money to this day, you may want to allocate a specific, reasonable pool of money for those particular expenditures. If you have trouble treating yourself (rather than your children or your spouse), then the money is earmarked for that. That has worked, in

Alyssa's case. "If you start to chip away at it, it's not unlike other areas that you've mastered," she says. "It's a skill."

Money Stories and How They Manifest Themselves

The goal of having you do all this work is to reach back and connect the dots for yourself. But I find sometimes it's helpful to see examples as well. So we asked financial therapists Amanda Clayman and Eric Dammann to help us lay out some of the most common money stories and to explain how they turn into common day-to-day behaviors and what you can do to begin dealing with them. Perhaps this will get your wheels turning.

~

Today's behavior: You need to control all the money in your family. You can't compromise with your spouse or partner on a financial plan, or how the family's budget should be allocated.

Possible origins: You had a parent who would take your money as a child, or there was some other loss or betrayal that makes it hard for you to trust and partner with somebody else. Or there was a domineering family member who controlled all the money, and that's how you learned to relate to money and others.

Potential next steps: Try carving out a small, safe space where your significant other can control the money. Maybe they pay a bill for a few months or handle a piece of the budget. If that goes well, it can help you ease into more of a financial partnership.

~

Today's behavior: You set a budget for yourself, but you always end up going over it in wildly dramatic ways.

Possible origins: You weren't allowed to have your needs met as a child, or to use money to have your needs met as a child. So now, you spend on yourself as a way of saying, "I exist, I deserve this." Denying yourself feels like denying that you're a person.

Potential next steps: Think of other ways you could have your needs met, other ways to take care of yourself. You could start exercising more, take up a hobby you've always been interested in, or try meditation. There are a variety of ways to indulge yourself and stake your claim as a person that don't cost a fortune to adopt.

~

Today's behavior: You can't look at your 401(k) or make any decisions about it. The idea of dealing with it gives you anxiety.

Possible origins: A parent was very domineering with money and never let you have control over it, so you don't feel you can control it now.

Potential next steps: This is essentially a money phobia, and you can treat it that way—by taking baby steps to address it. For instance, you might start by looking at your 401(k) statement or logging into your 401(k) account online. Regular appointments with a financial planner or financial therapist can help you take steps to make decisions about the account—slowly if necessary. The more you learn you can handle each step, the more confidence you'll have moving forward.

~

Today's behavior: You're extremely anxious about money, even though you have half a million dollars in the bank.

Possible origins: You grew up in a household in which there was a lot of anxiety about money, or in which some traumatic money event occurred—a parent's job loss, for instance—that created stress and struggle with finances.

Potential next steps: Tell yourself that the cause of your anxiety is your parents or family or childhood, not what's happening currently in your life. You are not doomed to repeat the mistakes of others. For instance, if your parents' money stress stemmed from debt, make a point to be debt-free (or on the road to get there). If a job loss caused all the anxiety, make a point to have a healthy emergency fund. The more you can shore up your own finances and show yourself that you're in a better position, the better you'll feel about things. And start keeping a gratitude journal. Every day, note three things that you're thankful for. Then, at the end of each week, go back and read over what you've written. You will start to notice a pattern of good things in and around your life.

~

What Happens When You Rewrite Your Story?

Is all of this work worth it? It absolutely can be.

Lisa's Money Story

My mom was a teacher and my dad an engineer, so we were by no means poverty stricken, but I often heard comments like: "Do you think money grows on trees?" Or, "We can't afford that." And, I come from the Midwest, and I think sometimes there's the mentality here that money is evil. As I grew older there was an awareness of that blueprint, but also a knowledge that it didn't have to be my standard as an adult with my own children.

My husband and I believed with hard work and personal development that we could challenge that. Part of it for me was realizing that it wasn't just my husband's income, that my income was potentially unlimited, depending on my ability to grow my own skills. I wanted to continue to challenge myself, and along with that came a higher paycheck. I am also a person of faith. I grew up in the church. [I dug into the question of whether there were] tones of: "You can't be a good Christian if you have wealth"? And really giving that some thought and some discernment, I realized if I want to be able to give abundantly, I have to earn abundantly. And I made the decision that money isn't a bad thing.

❦

Back to the Beginning

Which brings us back to Christine, whose money story you read at the beginning of the chapter. She, too, over the past few years, made a specific effort to dive into her money story and to make changes that improve the ways she—and her husband—are going about their day-to-day financial lives. They talk about money, she says, almost daily. Here's where she is now:

Christine's Money Story, Continued

[Over the past few years, my husband and I have made a lot of progress, learning to talk about money and work together with money. The result has been] kind of detaching myself from thinking the amount of money I make equals how important or valuable I am as a person. In the past, I would have a huge month and feel great about my life and then maybe have a smaller month and feel like I was worthless.

Doing the work means that something that would have previously been really stressful because I was equating it to myself has now become an external thing. The biggest piece is that how you feel about money is a choice. I really do believe that. And it doesn't mean it's easy or that it's going to happen overnight. But I think that is my biggest lesson, my biggest takeaway. It's about choosing to create what you feel about money and also what you do with it. When you talk about owning your money and owning your life . . . I've really found that the two are intertwined.

~

What Have We Learned

- *You have a money story. No one read it to you, or told it to you. You absorbed it and need to do a little work to understand it.*

- *You may behave in ways that line up with your story—or in complete opposition.*

- *You may have sought out a partner with a similar story or a completely different one—but understanding their story is key to your future happiness (and sanity).*

- *With work, you can rewrite this story to sync up with how you want to live your life today.*

Where Do We Go from Here

Money can be an emotional fuse causing us to make decisions or react in ways that don't make sense. Just like you need to understand your story, you need to understand your emotional tendencies with money in order to create the life and future you want.

CHAPTER 3

Why Is Money So Maddeningly Emotional?

Around the time of the recession, I was pretty good about saving. I was working at a newspaper. I saved almost $60,000. That was amazing and impressive and then, at the end of 2010, I had a really bad breakup. I was so emotionally devastated. I went through my savings like it was melting ice cream. I don't even know what I spent it on. It was drinks with friends, getting a whole new wardrobe because I let my ex get to me and he had made a comment about my clothes. I treated it like Monopoly money, like it's not real.

Recently, though, I was unemployed for a while. I started cleaning out my closet. When I looked into my closet, I wanted to throw up. Because that's not who I am, I'm more into helping other people and donating to good causes and travel. Plus, it was causing me to have anxiety to see this mess everywhere. That motivated me emotionally to say that I have enough stuff. I don't need three pink dresses that look almost exactly alike. My best friend says no lesson in life is free. The horror that I felt—the anxiety, the fear, is motivation enough for me to want to save more.

—Carmen, 30s, communications professional, New Jersey

~

On October 9, 2017, economist Richard Thaler, a professor at the University of Chicago Booth School of Business, won the Nobel Prize in

Economics. His name may sound familiar to you if you saw the movie *The Big Short* (he was the one sitting next to Selena Gomez at the poker table) or like to read best-seller lists, where his book *Nudge* spent some time in 2008. Thaler's prizewinning feat was a body of research documenting that—and explaining why—when it comes to making decisions about money (and also about life), human beings are irrational. We do things that don't make sense. Things that aren't logical. Things that are not in our best interest—small things, like not being willing to pay a little more for an umbrella when it's pouring outside, and big things, like not saving enough for retirement. And we do them consistently.

Thaler's work—along with that of psychologists Daniel Kahneman and Amos Tversky—gave birth to an entire discipline called behavioral economics, which Investopedia defines as "the study of psychology as it relates to the economic decision-making processes of individuals and institutions." That's fine for the ivory tower set. But I prefer to think of it as "the study of why smart people do stupid things with money."

Part of the answer is biology. We are hardwired—much like our caveperson ancestors—to be present focused rather than future focused. We still prefer immediate gratification to gratification that comes down the road. And we have a particularly hard time when down the road is so many years away that we can't even fathom what it will look like in reality. We know this because researchers have used MRIs to look at our brains in the process of making choices about money. They flash images of things we want, and they chart the activity in our heads. And what they see is that when something we want comes into view, the pleasure centers in our brains light up. When we actually get the reward, we get a rush of the feel-good chemical dopamine. (You can imagine this sort of purchase/reward scenario if you've ever gotten a jolt of excitement from buying something on sale.) The problem is, if you ask people to wait for the reward, it's very difficult to bring about the same sort of brain reaction. You typically have to make the reward much, much bigger in order to do it. And things that are far off in the future—like the retirement we're all told to save for—don't light up our brains at all.

So, biology doesn't help us. And then emotion—how we *feel* about these decisions, choices, issues, events—comes along and completely does us in.

Emotion is 90 percent humidity when you've traveled 500 miles and left your flat iron at home. You'd avoid it if you could, but it's here and it's happening and you have to deal with it instead.

Why is that? Again, it's largely biological. We are human. And human beings are emotional creatures. We not only feel what is happening in the moment, as we discussed in the last chapter, but we also filter those feelings through layer upon layer of what happened to us in the past.

The big problem with this is not that emotions are bad, but that emotions can cloud our judgment. When we are emotional, we are more focused on how we feel and not on what we think, says Dr. Linda Henman, an expert in decision-making under stress. "Logic makes us think, but emotions make us act. We make decisions that we sense will bring about an improved condition, even though we don't have the facts to back up that conclusion."

WHEN QUESTIONS DON'T HAVE ANSWERS, EMOTION REIGNS

One reason that money is so emotionally charged is that there are two distinct types of money questions. There are the ones that have correct answers.

- What's the best rewards credit card?
- Can I get a better deal on cable?
- Is it cheaper to buy or lease that car?

But there is a whole realm of financial questions for which correct answers simply don't exist.

- What's the best way to invest my retirement money?
- Will stocks go up or down next year?
- How long am I going to live?

With questions like these the possibility exists that you can do everything right and still not end up with the result you were going for. That's because of the little wild card called life. It forces us to deal with the unexpected: Layoffs. War. Illness. Floods. My pulse is rising just writing these words. I'm getting emotional and *they're not even happening*. That's how powerful uncertainty can be. It's a trigger for fear. The more uncertain the outcome, the more anxiety is produced. The more anxiety that's produced, the more irrational we become.

Now, of course, not everyone feels emotion in equal measure. There are some people who find uncertainty and ambiguity completely terrifying. There are others who can compartmentalize, worrying sometimes but not letting uncertain outcomes bother them at others. And then there are those who find uncertainty at the least interesting and at the most exciting. You know what these people are called? Men.

Bottom line, says psychologist Maggie Baker, is that it's not good: "Uncertainty amplifies impulsivity and risk taking in a way that usually doesn't work real well."

The F-Word (Not That One)

Of course, uncertainty is not the only factor driving these highly charged emotional bursts. We also bring our own set of personal expectations to the party.

The night before my college graduation, I had a long and somewhat boozy conversation on the porch of a West Philly row house with my friend Kevin. It was one of those "where do you think you'll be in five/ten/twenty years" conversations. I remember laying my whole life out for him in detail: engaged by 25, married by 26, first kid before 30, running a magazine by 35. He shook his head. "But how do you know?" he asked. "I just do," I told him, full of misguided confidence and Chardonnay.

The trouble is, when these expectations don't line up with our realities (a divorce, in my case, and a seismic shift in print journalism) the result is Frustration. With a capital *F*.

The key to dealing with this is *not* shutting down emotionally, but rather allowing yourself to recognize what's going on inside you. Psychologists explain that this is about awareness. Just as you can't change any behavior unless you're aware of what you're doing (see: tracking your spending or keeping a food diary), you can't deal with your emotions until you're aware of what they are and where they're coming from.

If You Can't Feel It, You Can't Change It

Julie, 30s, is a marketing analyst from Baltimore with an MBA. As the work she does might suggest, Julie is systematic in her office and her life. She meticulously planned her finances so that the very day her last car payment was due, the loans for her MBA would kick in. Then, this year, she and her fiancé bought a house, and all that excellent planning went right out the window. "This is the first time in my life that I have had a substantial amount of debt," Julie says. "I open Credit Karma every day and it gives me heart palpitations."

Despite those palpitations Julie is fortunate in that she is completely aware of a) her emotions and b) what's causing them. Many of us don't see as clearly. Recognizing those emotions—and the reactions that they tend to raise—takes practice. Actually doing the right thing as they swirl about takes both practice and perspective.

The good news is, you've already gotten good at not reacting emotionally in other parts of your life. Consider the calculus you go through when having an argument with your spouse—or even a heated discussion with your best friend. When your ire is up (because she was ten minutes late *again*, because he didn't put the cereal bowl in the dishwasher *again*, even though you've asked him *a hundred times*), the temptation to say things you regret later can be enormous. You want to say: *You never listen to me. You know how much this pisses me off.* And maybe even: *I'm done with you.*

But you don't.

Why not? Because you know that you may not be able to take those words back. Your goal in that moment is not to permanently damage your relationship. You *really* love your spouse. You *really, really* love your best friend. The unstated and unrealized goal is to temporarily hurt the other person because they did something that insulted you, or made you feel disrespected.

That's the tip-off. When there is no clear benefit to acting out in that way—to making that particular decision—it is a decision based more on emotion than on fact.

Emotions Can Rewind the Clock

It's also important to recognize that what's happening in the moment may in fact not be responsible for your emotions in that moment. The timing can be delayed, sometimes by hours but sometimes by years.

If we have a particularly bad day at work or don't receive an invite to a gathering when all our friends do, or if it takes thirty-five minutes for the parking garage to dig our car out of the lot, we have the ability to suppress our emotions. We put on our presentable, public faces. And then we get home and open the Visa bill only to see that our spouse spent $250 on a concert ticket (one he's seeing with his friends, by the way, not with us) and we lose it. We're not really mad at him (we've spent that much on things where he wasn't involved). We just need to let it out—and money-related matters are often the pressure valve that pops.

Other times our emotions are tied up in our money stories—in things that happened earlier in our lives. These often show up in life as trigger points. If you've made financial mistakes in the past—and you see yourself repeating those mistakes—it's time for some self-reflection to see what's setting you in motion. If criticism sends you to the mall, credit card at the ready—just like if criticism sends you to the freezer, spoon in hand—you need to recognize: When I am criticized, I spend money I don't really want to be spending. Or: When I am criticized, I overeat. Then go back to your story to try to discover the why. Did you see your mother shopping (or eating) in reaction to criticism from your father? Did she seem to feel better as a result?

The one-two punch of emotion + story can even disarm women who are both successful and have their financial houses in order, explains entrepreneurship coach Karen Southall Watts. "In the back of your mind is that little voice from when you were a child that says the mother denies herself the new dress to buy things for everyone else in the family. Or the good girlfriend postpones what she wants on the vacation so the boyfriend can go hang gliding." It's up to us to rein it in.

Money Is More Than What It Buys

But before we get into the how of managing all this emotion, we need to look at one other thing: Money, like no other resource, is not just linked to our survival—we need money to buy food, to pay for a place to live—but also to our social standing and our feelings of self-worth. Money largely determines our place in society, and it's a big deciding factor when it comes to who our peers are—who we want to and get to hang out with, who wants to and gets to hang out with us. "Wherever your target social group is—whether or not your financial situation matches up to that—is going to have a huge effect on your emotions," behavioral economist Sarah Newcomb explains. In other words, life turns out to involve playing a never-ending game of *Survivor*. And when we're booted off the island, emotions fly high.

It helps to keep remembering that we are, just like those cave-dwelling ancestors, tribal. And if the entire tribe packs up and moves away and we are left standing there (unless we are Matt Damon on Mars and we are a biologist who can grow potatoes in our own manure until Jessica Chastain comes back to rescue us), we die. And we are terrified of death.

All of which goes a long way to explaining the troublesome groupthink that leads to bad financial decision-making. It's not the flared jeans or uncomfortable modern couches you spent too much on because everyone else had them. There are examples of this in every market bubble and every market crash. "It's not greed [driving us]," says psychologist Brad Klontz. "It's fear of being all alone."

And it brings about a horrible cycle. When we're worried about our finances falling apart, we're worried about losing our status and our belonging. In other words, financial stress leads to survival stress. Which leads to health problems, which are expensive and lead to more financial problems, and the whole damn cycle starts over again.

But it doesn't have to. So let's take a look at a plan for recognizing what's happening, the emotions that result, and the behaviors that they can elicit. We may not be able to completely disentangle this mess, but we can make progress in that direction.

GETTING OFF THE EMOTIONAL ROLLER-COASTER

Step 1: Identify your triggers.

The first step to keeping your emotions from sabotaging your finances is to identify them. Are you angry? Scared? Guilty? Tired?

Okay, tired isn't officially an emotion. Tired is a feeling. Just like cranky is a mood. Because they all have the ability to impact our behavior with money, we're going to consider them all triggers here. Still, it may be helpful to know the difference, so . . .

Emotions are immediate physical responses—in the brain and the body—to what's happening in the moment. They take just fractions of a second, are hardwired and similar across most humans. Emotions bring on **feelings**, which are our mental and physical reactions. They differ from person to person because they are colored by our personal stories and experiences. And while emotions are fleeting, feelings last longer. But not as long as **moods**, which are based on things beyond emotions and feelings, including the weather, the light, our health, and our sleep. Moods can last hours, even days.

And although the research on whether women tend to experience emotions, feelings, and moods more deeply than men do is mixed, we do when it comes to the negative ones and particularly those about money. Here are some common triggers and the financial responses they tend to bring about.

Anger: Makes us more optimistic and more likely to take risks than we would naturally be.

Anxiousness or Anxiety: Makes us feel nervous about what's coming down the road—both short and long term. It can lead to oversaving, being too conservative, and not enjoying the day-to-day.

Fear: Elicits a fight-or-flight response because we're worried about survival. Can lead to bailing out of the markets when they're correcting, even though you've got plenty of time to weather the storm.

Desire: A deep longing for something that can lead to overspending when you can't afford it.

Embarrassment: Makes us want to crawl into a hole—preferably one that's dark and deep. It can result in not taking the appropriate actions to protect and improve your own finances, whether asking to pay less at a group dinner where you just had an appetizer or asking for a raise.

Guilt: Remorse at having wronged others by doing something you know was hurtful—or winning when others lose. We often react by spending way too much on them to compensate.

Happiness: Like anger, makes us more likely to take financial risks than we otherwise would be. In this case, because we're feeling so buoyant.

Jealousy: When you want what someone else has. Leads to buying things you can't afford and racking up debt.

Regret: A close cousin of shame. Remorse over making a bad decision in the past can prevent you from taking action in the present. If you regret that you didn't start saving younger, you have trouble starting because you feel it's too late.

Sadness: Feels like a big void—a physical hole somewhere around your heart. We often try to plug that void by buying stuff.

You want to get to the point where you can tie how you're feeling to what you're doing. Sadness and anger are particularly good places to start because they're such clear feelings with very clear ties to specific behaviors. The last few times you felt sad or angry, what did you do to deal with those feelings? Now, flip the question. The last few times you felt emotional about money, what had happened in your life to get you there? Sometimes it helps to involve another person in your introspection. A friend. A spouse. They may be able to see you more clearly than you see yourself.

The last big money fight I had with my husband is an example of that. In order for this story to make sense, you should know that this is the second marriage for both of us. And, though we have a joint household account, we haven't otherwise merged our finances. Anyway, my husband—who is eight years older than I am—was about to retire from his job of twenty years. He made some sort of offhand comment about how he'd saved so well that even if he didn't earn anything for the next four years, we'd be okay. He wouldn't have to start tapping into his retirement. He wouldn't have to take more from me.

And I lost it. Not immediately, but bit by bit. I dug into the numbers of how much it costs us to live, what I pay for and what he pays for—and how his savings wouldn't go as far as he thought and that maybe he should do some consulting. It devolved from there. But let me just say that ugly crying—on my part—was involved.

Though I was still smarting the next day when he came home, I was ready to let it go. That's when he told me the fight wasn't really about money at all. The fight was about independence—specifically mine. I work a lot. I like to work a lot. I don't want anyone questioning how much I work. His take was that when he stopped working, I was terrified that he was going to want me to, say, go out to lunch or an afternoon movie, things that would threaten my ability to work. So, I was pushing him to continue to earn to get him to continue to work so that I could do the same.

Pretty good for a guy with a BA in political science.

Talking about money is, unfortunately, harder than it should be. A

2014 study from Wells Fargo says that for 44 percent of Americans it's harder than politics, religion, even death. But give it a go anyway. If you can't do it with your spouse, try a friend. And if you can't talk, journal. Start making notes of these emotional periods and your financial actions. That may be what you need to do to spot the links.

Step 2: Give yourself permission to feel that way (but not to act on it).

Once you're starting to get a grip on the emotions/feelings/moods that drive particular actions, you can start trying to separate them. The idea is to allow yourself to have the feelings while keeping your finances moving in the right direction. How?

First, acknowledge that they have a right to be there. We have been told by teachers and parents to think logically about money and take emotions out of it. *Not possible.* We can't pretend that our financial decisions aren't woven up in all of our dreams. What we can do is take a look at the underlying need that we're meeting with our financial strategies, then see whether it's a healthy strategy to meet that need.

Perhaps you're feeling insecure or lonely and so you raise your hand for the spa weekend with the group of women you want to be closer to. It's more money than you wanted to spend and you're not really a massage person, but you do it anyway. Ask yourself: Is this sustainable? Are there ways I can do that without a) spending as much money and b) taking part in an activity I don't really enjoy? You can start to take emotions out of it when you recognize that you're using money to serve emotional purposes—but there are other ways to solve the problem as well.

It's also important to forgive yourself for letting those emotions mess you up in the past. Regret is one of the least helpful emotions when it comes to finances—and life. It's what gets in the way of calling the friend you were supposed to call last week, then a few days ago, then yesterday. When you feel so bad about not doing it, it makes it that much harder to pick up the phone. And it's what gets in the way of not hiring the financial advisor, not juicing up your savings, not making so many of the money moves we wish we had made before. Channel Elsa. Let it go. Then take one step in the right direction. Quickly e-mail a financial advisor you've been wanting to meet. That e-mail will put a dialogue into motion and you're off to the races.

Another way to manage emotions—not eliminate them, but manage them—is to change your framework. Let's go back to jealousy. We're jealous because other people have what we want—big things like great careers and wonderful relationships, but also small ones like the ability to do a headstand in yoga class and great hair. It would be best if you could avoid these comparisons (research has shown that people who can steer clear are happiest). But that's a tall order. So, instead, encourage yourself to compare down rather than up—with the Joneses on the left, who have the adorable but smaller house without the extra bay in the garage, not with the Joneses on the right, who have the palace with the moat. Do that, and you'll feel happier.

Income, by the way, plays a huge role here. Where people feel they stand in their community affects them on a daily basis. If you plant yourself in a neighborhood of seven-figure earners while you're in the sixes, life is going to be more stressful than it has to be, as Tracey, 30s, a lawyer and mom of two in New York, figured out. She recognizes there is a considerable amount of stress they put on themselves because they want to climb the ladder to that next step. Maybe, in hindsight, a starter home on a less affluent street would have been the way to go.

Step 3: Slow down.

Remember the difference between emotions, feelings, and moods is largely time based. And it's the emotions that drive us to act. So once you become aware of the fact that your emotional brain is driving many if not most of your behaviors, then you can build in a little time between the emotion and the action. And the fact that the emotion will have subsided during that time will often result in not taking the action at all.

So, you've had the big fight, like I had with my husband, which leads to getting angry which leads to wanting to act out which leads to the computer, where you do a significant amount of damage on Net-a-Porter. Here's my suggestion: Put all the stuff you want in your cart. But don't buy it. Or, maybe the trigger/result was a different one—maybe the stock market fell 2,000 points in a day and you decided you want to bail. Figure out what steps you would need to take to make that happen. Then don't. Whatever it is, sleep on it. Give yourself a good twenty-four hours—in shopping we call this a purchasing pause—for the emotions to subside. The stuff will still be in your cart in the morning. The stock market will still be open for business.

Essentially, you're editing your own behavior. It's easy when you're excited—or angry or frustrated or otherwise overly emotional—about something to become overconfident in what you're doing and miss the things that are not to your advantage. When you give yourself time to reflect, you get to a place where they don't sound quite as good.

Step 4: Retake control.

What does nervous feel like? Pulse racing. Adrenaline pumping. Hunger evaporating. Palms a little sweaty.

What does excited feel like? Pulse racing. Adrenaline pumping. Hunger evaporating. Palms a little sweaty.

Yet one is significantly better than the other. And research conducted by Alison Wood Brooks at Harvard Business School has shown that you can choose which feeling to recognize. Telling yourself, "I'm not nervous (or anxious, if that's how it manifests for you), I am excited," may—with a little fake-it-till-you-make-it practice—be enough to actually make you excited, rather than nervous.

This advice flies in the face of what you're typically told when you're nervous or anxious, which is: Calm down. Calming down is hard because it's the opposite of what you're feeling. Transitioning to the happier-yet-similar emotion of excitement is much easier. And Brooks's research showed that this change of mind gets you out of that space where you ruminate on all the possible bad outcomes and into one where you can focus on all the things that could go right. Participants in her studies who tried it performed better at public speaking, at karaoke, even on math tests.

Another form of changing your mind is to recognize that emotions can be used to impact our finances in a positive way. Money coach Christine Luken encourages her clients to do what she calls emotionally charged saving. The idea is to imagine, in the greatest—most emotional—detail possible what you're saving for and how it'll feel when you get it. How will it feel when you know, without a doubt, that your money will last as long as you will? How will it feel when you've paid off that mortgage? This works for short-term goals like big vacations, but it works particularly well for the longer-term ones that are so hard to reach because they're so squishy.

Finally, you can change your mind by making moves to retake control where you feel shaky. Tracking your finances is one such move. For Katrina, 30s, a life coach from Minnesota, tracking gives her "a sense of empowerment" because she's aware of what she has at any point in time. This system has bailed her out of more than one emotional jam. Among her assets, Katrina counts a town house in Atlanta that she rents out for income. When her most recent tenants were moving out, Katrina received a call from the property manager notifying her that the updates she was planning to make before leasing it out again were going to cost her triple the original estimate. At first, she was not just annoyed but agitated. Then she turned to her spreadsheet and she was able to figure out not just that she had the money, but where the money was going to come from. "I felt a sense of calm about it," she says.

And even if tracking is not your cup of tea, making other moves that insinuate you're in control of your money, your money is not in control of you, will temper your emotional swings. As behaviorist Sarah Newcomb's research showed: "In every income class, the people that believe they're in the driver's seat financially were significantly happier. They're having much more positive experiences, even if they're making less than $25,000 per year."

What Have We Learned

- *It's pretty much impossible to remove emotions from money.*

- *We're better off learning to recognize our emotions and what they are likely to trigger us to do, rather than separate them from our actions.*

- *There are four steps you can take to put yourself back in control.*

Where Do We Go from Here

Getting a grip on your own story and your own baggage solves part of the issue, but we also have to play well financially with others—spouses, partners, siblings, parents, friends. We'll delve into the complications of our money and our relationships.

⌒

CHAPTER 4

Your Money and Your Relationships

*My husband and I were in debt, and I felt out of control
because I didn't feel like I was responsible for it. We were
refinancing [the house over and over] and he was handling all
the bills and sort of floundering with his career. I remember
saying to my father: "I am never ever going to get out of this
financial hole. Ever." And my father said to me: "You're the one.
You are the one that is going to have to pull yourself out of this.
You can do it."*

*At the time I did not think it was possible. But fast-forward
ten years, and I'm financially secure. When we sold the house,
I used that money to pay off my half of the $100,000 credit card
debt. My [now] ex-husband said to me: "Oh my God, how did
you do that?" Because the way he deals with finances is vastly
different than me. And I said to him, "I am never, ever going
to be in financial debt again. I will never be paying the $25 a
month just so I don't have to pay the $10,000 that's owed." It's
probably what tore us apart.*

—Anna, 50s, lawyer, Philadelphia

⌒

Money and relationships can be a volatile combination. I'm not going
to overwhelm you with statistics. There are plenty that back up that
statement while also confirming the fact that your financial life is *insep-
arable* from your relationships. If you are feeling stress in your primary

love relationship, money is likely at the heart of it. The more tension you have around money, the more likely you are to split. And if you do break up, you're likely to say money was a top—if not the top—cause.

That makes sense. Even if you've gotten a handle on your own money issues, throwing another person with their own issues into the mix changes things. As Sara, 30s, a university administrator who recently moved in with her boyfriend, explains:

> *We'll go out to dinner and he orders the nice bottle of wine and three appetizers. I get nervous. We talk about buying a home. What he has in mind and what I have in mind are two different things. I don't need to have a Gucci-whatever and drive a Lexus. That's not important to me. [What's important to me] is just being financially secure.*

Sometimes, the differences between partners lead to meeting more or less in the middle. "I've always been a planner," says Julie, 30s, a marketing analyst from Baltimore. "I'm type A. I think ahead. I plan for worst-case scenarios, so I don't have to scramble when something comes up." Her fiancé is the opposite. "He is a spender—an experience-first kind of guy. He works hard and he wants to treat himself." After a little push and pull, they came to a happy medium. **"He pushed me to use what I worked so hard to create, I pushed him to think a little bit ahead. I tightened his bootstraps and he loosened mine."**

But other times, these differences are more oil and water than oil and vinegar. They add a layer of complication—and stress. Angela, 50s, a financial services executive from Wisconsin, worries because her wife is very reluctant to engage with their money at all. Angela is the primary breadwinner, but she wants her spouse involved. Still, whenever the topic comes up, her wife finds other things to busy herself with. "If something happens to me"—Angela shakes her head—"she wouldn't know what to do." And Riki, 40s, from Arizona, says that whenever the topic of money comes up with her husband, he freaks out. "He goes from zero to panic in two seconds." The result is that money is just not a conversation in their home. "We rarely talk about it," she says. "Never."

That is exactly what we're trying to avoid.

IN THE BEGINNING

The first three chapters of this book were devoted to understanding our financial selves. But successfully incorporating another person into your life means making the effort to understand them as well.

This may not seem important in the butterflies phase of a relationship. Then, differences seem charming, quirks seem cute, and the $1,500 he spent to wire the back deck for sound (when he could have spent one-tenth of that on a portable speaker) was a demonstration of how comfortable he wanted guests to be in his home. He's *evolved*, you thought, not *excessive*.

It's *because* things are so good that we don't establish boundaries about how finances will be handled. But over time, the glow fades. Your spouse or partner behaves in ways that you don't agree with, and the lack of clear rules or guidelines leads to tension, stress, and arguments. "Because money is a core survival issue, when people begin to feel fearful or that they might be taken advantage of, they lash out in unconstructive, unhealthy ways with their partner," says Deborah Price, founder of the Money Coaching Institute. And there goes the goodwill in your relationship.

These changes don't happen overnight. They may result from the course your lives together take. Erica, 40s, a lawyer and mother of three in California, always wanted to be able to support herself fully and independently. After law school, she took a job with a salary that grew to over six figures in just a few years. She didn't marry until she was 31 and when she did, she outearned her husband, which enabled her to amass the down payment for the house they eventually bought. "I felt comfortable and confident," she says.

But over the last twenty years, Erica stopped working. "My husband is a financial guy," she says. "Over time, he took over more and more of our finances [until] he'd assumed everything. And I was bothered by it. But at some point, I was busy working and then with the kids, and I just surrendered. Now, I've missed fifteen years and I don't feel confident. And I wonder, could I manage it? Could I manage it as well as he does?"

Often, the evolution in our relationships is so rapid and so exciting—*We're engaged...I'm pregnant. It's a girl!*—that we forget to talk about all of the other changes that happen as a result. Then we wake up and wonder: *How did I get here from there?*

That's what happened to Susan, 40s, a stay-at-home mother of two in California. "It's complicated when you're not contributing. There is this imbalance of power," she says. "These tiny little financial moments, where if [my husband] feels any financial stress, he'll take control over making the decisions because he's the one who pays for it. And I have to push back and remind him that this is a partnership and it's not his money solely. But the instant reaction is that it *is* his. And that's scary, too."

Susan (and the noted philosopher Avril Lavigne) are right. It *is* complicated.

That's why it's so important to understand not just *that* you and your partner are different, but *why* you're so different. You may feel like your husband is highly reactive, Price says. But, if you don't understand what it was like for him when he was growing up—how money was tight, for instance—you can't figure out what's driving his moods and outbursts today. It's easy to see a man who flies off the handle when the topic of money comes up as a bully. The reality may be that he's scared. "Context is very important," she says. "Especially for couples."

Planning a Time to Talk

If you think about communication as a continuum from total secrecy to complete transparency, many couples would be distinctly left of center. Sometimes it's not just that we don't want to talk about money, it's also that we don't know how. But if you're not talking about your money with your partner, you're really not talking about your life. Which is why many financial experts (and I have done this myself occasionally) suggest the concept of "money dates."[4] Some call these get-togethers money huddles or powwows or even (unfortunately) playdates. They're all attempts to make these conversations sound so enticing that you actually have them. The more years I write about money, the more I think the words *money date* sound completely ridiculous.

But I'm good with the concept. My husband and I make appointments to talk about money.

Why? Because one of us— *ummm, me*—doesn't really like to have them. Yes, I write and talk and communicate about money *for a living* and I don't particularly like to do it with my spouse. So, I don't expect that it's especially easy for you, either—which is not the same as saying it's okay to blow it off. Here's how to do it.

☞ And while we're on the topic of "money dates," if you're in the fledgling days of a relationship, I don't think it's necessary to stage a big reveal of your credit report or score before your first kiss or roll in the sack. As you start thinking about whether this is a person you could build a life with, you'll road test your common ground on career, family, religion, etc. This is when you start talking about money. If the fact that one of you is still paying off student loans or the other is expected to join the family business hasn't come up before, it should then.

EXERCISE 4

The Framework for Your Conversations

Pick a time. Too many money conversations aren't real conversations but rather offhand comments as one of you is heading out the door. Instead, plan time when you're not feeling pressured or put-upon. Weekend afternoons work in my house because there's usually a lull between exercise and errands and dinner with friends. Long car rides work, too. You don't want a lot of distractions.

Give yourself a big enough window. For us, thirty minutes is usually enough. Scott and Bethany Palmer of TheMoneyCouple.com suggest forty-five: fifteen to check in on recent spending and saving moves, fifteen for upcoming financial needs, and fifteen for future dreams. Spend at least a couple of minutes on what's going well. Sometimes we get so consumed with the negative that we forget to say, "Thank you, honey, for spending hours evaluating sixteen different air conditioner systems, poring over *Consumer Reports*, and saving us $5,000. I still don't know the difference between a condenser and a compressor, but I appreciate you doing all that work."

Listen, reflectively. When your other half says something, take it in. Process it. Then repeat it back to make sure you accurately got the gist of what was said. Don't offer a solution or an apology. Your job is to make the other person feel heard. This provides a forum for your partner to explore their own thoughts and feelings. Then let them do the same for you.

Breathe. These conversations can bring about rising heart rates, sweaty palms, and the desire to up and run. Breathe. Inhale slowly through your nose, holding for a count of three, then exhale slowly through your mouth. Repeat. Meditation, affirmations, and prayers can help, too.

Talk life before numbers. The overarching goal of these conversations is to get on the same page about what you want to do with this life you're living together—and how to make that happen. So, allow yourself to dream aloud. "What would it look like to spend an entire month in the mountains? We could ski/snowshoe/hike every day. Maybe we could rent an Airbnb with a wood-burning stove!" Once you've got a plan, you can start backing into the logistics and cost.

~

FIND A SYSTEM THAT WORKS FOR YOU

What's the best way of managing money in a relationship? Yours, mine, and ours accounts? Merging everything? Keeping everything separate? Yes. Yes. And yes. Seventy-seven percent of American couples share at least one bank account, according to Bankrate. But I firmly believe there isn't just one right way to do this. If your system is working, it's the right one for you.

For Christina, 30s, from Seattle, dividing conquers. She met her husband at age 18 and they've always kept separate finances. "I saw my parents fight about money, and it wasn't something I wanted in my relationship," she says. "I've always made a lot more than he does, so I never wanted to get into an issue of 'I bought this' or 'he bought that.' I don't want him to be insecure about that at all."

Maureen, 30s, a media director in LA, keeps her finances separate from her fiancé's, too. But they divvy up the bills based on the calendar. "My fiancé gets paid at a different time than me, so I will handle money at the beginning of the month, and he picks up when he gets paid and then we even out," she says. "It's very fluid."

Riki, 40s, the Arizona freelancer, merges some but not all. She watched as a friend, an older woman who had ceded control of the finances, lost her husband and was left penniless. "She assumed all those years that they had savings, they had insurance. The house wasn't even paid off. It was harrowing to see," she says. "We need to take care of ourselves."

Gina, 30s, a market research consultant in North Wales, Pennsylvania, merged everything with her husband because keeping things separate got too complicated. "We were getting into fights because we didn't know what the other person was doing. Combining everything—the bank accounts are linked—gave us complete transparency at all times."

Transparency is also the key to financial stability for Virginia, 30s, a freelancer with an irregular income in New York. "There are points in the year where I panic because [income is] in a lull. And then six paychecks come in the next week." Her solution: constant communication. She and her husband keep a running e-mail thread that bounces back and forth every time a paycheck lands. "And, we try to have a budget meeting every few months," she says.

And then there's Lindsay, 50s, a senior executive at a jewelry company in San Francisco. When she met her husband two decades ago, they chose *not* to merge their money. "Because he made more, he paid more. But I always felt like: 'I'm spending this amount of money to get my eyebrows done and it's not his business. He never needs to know.'" And that was the way it went, until they had their first child. Lindsay spent the next eight and a half years as a stay-at-home mom, not earning a penny. "My husband said, 'Pick a number and I'll just dump it in your bank account as if you were working. And then you just keep doing whatever you're doing.' So, I had an allowance—which sounds so retro—but it worked beautifully for us." They based the number on how much Lindsay was making before she stopped working—about $2,000 a month. She paid for all the kids' stuff, her clothes, groceries, and gas. He picked up the big stuff, the mortgage, cars, vacations. "I liked it because I never had to ask and I could plan on how I was going to use the money," she recalls. "And even when I wasn't earning, we had no conflict about money."

I hope you noticed a couple of threads in these examples. First, they are all different—and yet they are all successful. Second, the system you start with may not be the one you have today or that you finish up with. Just as Gina and Lindsay have changed the ways they've managed money through the years, my husband and I have recently been talking about whether we're due to switch things up.

Ours, as I mentioned, is a second marriage—for both of us. When we married, he had kids in college and was spending a lot more than I was. Today, his kids are out, mine are in, and my bills are significantly higher than his. Initially, we kept everything separate and just split up the household and other joint bills proportional to our incomes. But, eventually, that system got on my nerves. I didn't like having to remember who paid for dinner the last time so that we could alternate. So, we got a joint credit card, opened a joint checking account (to pay that card), and started using those vehicles to pay some other household expenses as well.

The secret ingredient in making any and all of these systems work? Autonomy. As Lindsay said so perfectly, *"I'm spending this amount of money to get my eyebrows done and it's not his business. He never needs to know."* Bingo. The albatross in your spending may be your sushi habit, birthday lunches for your best friends, or something else that matters more to you than it does to the joint holder of your Visa. And vice versa.

If you can give each other breathing space—and spending freedom— while comingling all of your accounts, terrific. If you can't, make some or all of your accounts separate or create a stash that's specifically for autonomous spending. That's what married financial advisors Marlow (a woman) and Chris (a man) Felton have done. A snippet of our conversation with them:

> MARLOW: *We're two individuals with two different upbringings, but we wouldn't be able to work together cohesively as a couple if we didn't understand what drives each other. For example, my husband has this need to be liked.*

CHRIS: *No, I don't.*

MARLOW: *Yes, you do. He likes people to like him. I like people to respect me. Because of his need to be liked, I've seen him overspend at bars because he wants to buy everyone the round of drinks.*

CHRIS: *People pleasing was a root of a lot of our challenges. I had to do certain things and to look a certain way. I had to have a certain house, a certain car. It's an approval addiction and it's pretty powerful. It was the root of the financial challenges I faced back in the day.*

MARLOW: *Without the awareness [of his background], I get mad at Chris; Chris is frustrated because I am mad at him; and the whole thing blows up. [But I was also] tired of hiding shoes in the trunk of my car when I went to the mall. I'd wait until he was gone and bring them in the closet and hope he didn't notice. I thought this was ridiculous, and it wasn't going to be good for our relationship long term. I didn't like the way it felt.*

Their solution was to create what they call a "fun fund"—an equal amount of money that gets deposited into individual accounts for discretionary purposes each month. For Chris, the fun fund means if he wants to buy everyone a round of drinks, that's fine, but he only has a certain number of dollars to do it. For Marlow, it means she can plunk her shopping bags on the counter with no second thoughts. He calls it "ingenious." She says it's "the most important thing" they've done. (P.S. It was her idea.)

And while we're talking about autonomy hacks, I'm a fan of the arbitrary spending limit. Essentially you come up with a number—$50, $500, $5,000, $50,000, whatever makes sense based on your resources and your tolerance for giving up control—and agree that neither of you is going to spend or invest that much money without discussing it first. Discussing, by the way, doesn't mean asking for permission, but it also doesn't mean that you can drop it in a text and pass GO.

Then, stick with that system until you *both* agree to a change. This is important. Every year, usually around Valentine's Day—because why not ruin a nice holiday involving chocolate and flowers—I receive at least one and sometimes several new studies on the topic of *financial infidelity,* which is when you keep secrets about money from your spouse. A 2018 version from CreditCards.com noted that one in five romantic partners has (or used to have) a credit card or bank account that their significant other doesn't know about. This is true despite the fact that about one-third of the people currently in a relationship believe that lying in this way about money is worse than cheating physically.

If you're among those secret keepers, it's time to come clean. This is one of those Nixonian scenarios where the cover-up is worse than the crime. It is perfectly acceptable to a) want to have and b) actually have money that is yours alone. It's when you're discovered to be lying about it or telling other lies to hide its existence that you start going down the rabbit hole that can ruin your relationship.

Just think about the conclusions you might jump to if you discovered your spouse was hiding a bank account from you. The mind very quickly hurtles from good (*it's because he wants to throw me a surprise party for my 40th*) to bad (*maybe he has a gambling habit I don't know about*) to worse (*he has another wife and three kids living in Albuquerque*). Save yourself the trouble. Tell your partner that you have it. Explain why you're keeping it. Offer him or her the option to do the same.

One more thing before we move on from this discussion of systems. Having joint bank accounts doesn't excuse you from two accounts you *must* maintain individually. One is a credit card account—a bank card, not a store one—on which you are the primary cardholder. You need this because of the big Ds: Death and Divorce. If your spouse dies or you split up and you don't already have credit in your own name, it may be tough to get it. Save yourself the trouble.

The second is a retirement account. Not having one means you're leaving valuable tax breaks on the table. More importantly, having stocks, bonds, and other investments of your own makes it much more likely that you'll be interested in—one could even say *invested in*—managing them.

Bringing in Help If You Need It

Perhaps you've been nodding along through this chapter thinking: *I can try that.* But maybe you're thinking: *Yeah, and when I wake up tomorrow I'll have skin like Salma Hayek's and Keith Urban in my bed.* If you're in the latter category, you may decide you need professional help. That's the conclusion Ashley, 40s, a therapist from California, came to:

> *My husband has very strong opinions about the economy and where it's headed. He believes that everything is going to go to hell in a handbasket. I've always taken this backseat. I figured: I'll let him do it. He's smart. I also realized he has this psychology around money that's very powerful. And I wasn't willing to challenge him on it. Yes, I was busy raising children and going to graduate school, but those are just excuses. Finally, I become more of an adult and tried to step up, and it's been a big issue in our marriage. The tension around it. The power dynamic. I felt very powerless, like I should defer to him. So, I decided I need someone who can help me talk to him. I hired this financial/business coach, she's kind of like a therapist. She keeps me accountable and lets me cry on the phone. We meet every month and she's helped me get my arms around my business and my personal life, too.*

Hiring help to iron out the financial kinks (for lack of a better word) in your relationship is not anything to feel embarrassed about or blame yourself for. If you want to place blame, send it society's way. We've got decades of an ingrained cultural dynamic where men are taught the road to respect is to assert their independence, while women get the message that it comes through supporting others. If you can't get yourself to step up, a financial advisor or a therapist can be hugely helpful.

Carol, 60s, a recent retiree from North Carolina, says she and her husband have utilized one for years. Carol never really enjoyed or felt comfortable in financial conversations—but she didn't want to dig her head in the sand, either. Involving their advisor in their interactions—essentially talking "through" the advisor—has enabled her and her husband of almost twenty years to manage their money more calmly and rationally. "The fact that he's a neutral third party takes the emotion out of it." And that, as Martha Stewart would say, is a very good thing.

Money Complicates Other Relationships, Too

When we talk about relationships, our significant others get a lot of airtime, with family running a close second. Yet, it's our friendships that have the best chance of improving our health and happiness throughout our adult lifetimes, a 2017 study from Michigan State University found. And money has the ability to do a number on those as well. Nearly half of consumers say money is a cause of friendship stress, according to a Bank of America survey. That stress comes as much or more from inside us—and how we react to what's happening in the lives of our friends—than it does from the interactions between us.

It happens when you're the one with less money. "When all my friends started buying houses, I felt like we were behind," says Julie, 30s, the marketing analyst from Baltimore. "There was a point where every other day someone on social media was posting a house with a SOLD sign out front. I started thinking that maybe I should be buying a house."

But it also happens when you're the one with more. Leisa Peterson and her husband became real estate millionaires in their 30s. Once they had the money, they felt they had to live a life that showed their success—so they built a house that was bigger and grander than anyone else in their social set had at the time. When they moved in, everything changed. "People felt uncomfortable," says Peterson, who now (not coincidentally) works as a money coach. "They treated us differently when they came for dinner. I remember thinking, 'Oh my gosh what have we done?' We hadn't changed and I assumed that everyone knew we hadn't changed, but people didn't come back. It was heartbreaking." Eventually the couple made new friends with people who hadn't known them before the house. But, Peterson still says, "My life fell apart when I got all that money."

And sometimes it even happens when you *think* a friend has more or less, even when in reality they don't. Money coach Emily Shutt spent years working in consulting before opening her practice. She was earning a nice salary but was still not keeping up with her friends who were buying cars and taking splashy vacations. "I had one friend who ordered a custom BMW," Shutt remembers. "She tracked it as it shipped over from Germany. I thought she must have been making so much money because there was no way I could afford that car." Months after the car arrived, the friend mentioned how she hoped to earn $70,000 that year. Shutt was floored. "I realized that I had, for years, been earning more money than her," she says. "We were just seeing money very differently."

EXERCISE 5

KEEP YOUR FINANCES FROM MESSING UP YOUR FRIENDSHIPS

- **Accept your reality.** When you chose your career path, you did it knowing what the income trajectory would likely be. Your friends did the same. It's not fair—or healthy—to blame the surgeon who spent four years in med school and eight in residency for the fact that she has a bigger house. Similarly, if you're the surgeon, there's a line between treating your writer best friend once in a while and becoming patronizing.

- **It's easier if you can open up a bit.** Four in five women say they've refrained from talking about money with someone they're close with, according to Fidelity research. Half say it's too personal. A third say it's uncomfortable. They're right. But if you can get over the hurdle, it encourages others to do the same with you. Figuring out what your financial goals are and then sharing them with the people closest to you allows you to gracefully back away from the pricey group vacation. Opening the door as to why you're saying no allows your friends to accept it.

- **Embrace the "Imperial We."** As you plan—and before you go to—events, have an active discussion, putting the emphasis on the group. Where do *we* want to go? How much do *we* want to spend? Do *we* think it's worth it?

Finally, know that all friendships aren't going to last—but the ones that do will be better ones. Statistically, women increase their numbers of friends through age 25, then we pare back—but in favor of fewer, higher quality relationships, according to researchers in Finland and the UK. So be consistent with the people that matter most to you. And focus on what you still have in common rather than focusing on the differences.

What Have We Learned

- *Money has the ability to wreak more havoc in our relationships than pretty much anything else, so it's important to establish a framework to deal with it.*

- *Setting specific times and processes for talking about money is hugely helpful. If you find you can't do this, hire a financial advisor or therapist to help you get going.*

- *There is no one right way to manage the family money or set up accounts; if it works for you, it works.*

Where Do We Go from Here

Now that you're more aware of who you are as a financial being (and who you're partnered up with), you can be more effective in dealing with the tactical, practical elements of your money. In the next section, we'll tackle getting paid what you're worth before moving on to investing, building a business (or side hustle), buying real estate, and using your money in ways that make you happy.

PART II

You in Control of Money: Making the Most of the Resources You Have

CHAPTER 5

Getting Paid What You're Worth...
Plus Tax

I just got a little raise. I make $66,000 now, and I was offered $64,000. Before I was starting, they told me their budget was sixty to seventy [thousand], so I knew there was $70,000 [available but] I didn't push for that. I think I have that same thing other women have; I have imposter syndrome and I'm uncomfortable talking about money.

— Kristin, 30s, social media manager, Vermont

My company was a small company, so I didn't negotiate for raises as often as I would have liked to. I knew approximately what we were making and what the partners were making (at times they weren't taking a paycheck). For me to ask for a raise... I don't know... I didn't want to seem greedy or that I didn't appreciate that we were all working hard. I went from full-time to part-time, and I felt I am not getting a raise, but I'm getting all these other benefits and a flexible work schedule and I'm okay with that. The benefits to me were as important as money.

— Elissa, 40s, management consultant, Ohio

In early 2018, I recorded a podcast with MSNBC's Mika Brzezinski, *Morning Joe* cohost and author of the best-selling book *Know Your*

Value. I took a breath before launching in and glanced down at my show notes—which always have some statistics or thoughts that my producer, Kelly Hultgren, has prepped to get me going. One sentence stood out: *I saw a headline recently that said American women are finally earning 80 cents on the dollar compared to men.* This was supposed to be good news. It wasn't 78 cents any longer, or even 79. It was 80. And I looked at Mika and said: "I am so sick of this. Aren't you sick of this?" She replied, "Yes, and I'm doing something about it."

We all have to—and that's the point of this chapter.

Getting paid is good. Getting paid more is better. Combating anxiety about asking for what we're worth means understanding the pay gap—where it comes from and why it still exists. But it also means getting a grip on why many of us still feel ambivalent (sometimes guilty) about earning more money, having more money, and helping other women to do the same. We have to help other women as friends, as colleagues, even as employers. (I recently gave a woman on my team a raise, then a week later gave her another one. Why? Because the work she was doing was worth another $5,000 a year—I knew that and felt she needed to know it, too.)

Why the Salary Gap Persists

A little bit of history: A little over thirty years ago, women earned 64 cents for every dollar a man earned—a pay gap of 36 cents. Today, we earn 80 cents, making the gap 20 cents[5] or about half what it used to be.

For women of color, the gap is even larger. Black women earn 63 cents for every dollar men do. Hispanic women, 54 cents. Asian women are the exception to the rule, earning 87 cents for every dollar a man makes. Why are there such dramatic racial differences? Entire

☞ Gaps are calculated slightly differently depending on the data set you use. The Bureau of Labor Statistics doesn't count bonuses while the Census Bureau does, and some calculations are based on hourly wages while others are based on salaries. Confusing, yes. The important thing to know: it's still there and it's still big.

books have been written on the subject, but my friend Stacey Tisdale, a fellow financial journalist and author, gave me the CliffsNotes version for black women over salads and omelettes at a local French bistro.

She explained, you've got to start back when Abraham Lincoln freed the slaves. Lincoln set up the Freedman's Savings and Trust Company, commonly called the Freedman's Bank, which was supposed to allow blacks to save and learn about money after slavery. In less than a decade, black people saved $57 million, which would be worth more than $6 trillion in today's dollars. They never saw the money. Some of it was misinvested. Some, Tisdale recounts, was stolen and used to build the Treasury Annex building in Washington, DC. The bank failed. And the depositors were never reimbursed (though in 2015 Treasury secretary Jacob Lew renamed the building the Freedman's Bank Building and said it should "serve as a reminder . . . for greater financial inclusion for all Americans"). The Freedman's Bank wasn't the only slight. Ninety years of Jim Crow laws enforced racial segregation, which kept blacks from educational and economic strides. Redlining limited the availability of financial services in neighborhoods where black people lived, effectively cutting them out of the housing market and off from the primary way Americans built wealth. There was much more, but you get the idea. Other races and cultures have fought their own battles and have their own scars. But in each case, Tisdale points out: "You then have to layer onto all of this that we're women."

Closing the Gap Slooooowly

What's shrinking the gap, albeit like molasses? The progress of younger women, who first gained educational equality with men—then surpassed them. More young women are also choosing higher paying, traditionally male-dominated fields (coding, finance, law). By 2012, young women entering the workforce earned 93 cents for every dollar a man earned.

Unfortunately, those gains aren't particularly sticky. As some women leave the workforce to care for kids or older parents, or search for increased work-life flexibility, the gap opens right back up again. According to the American Association of University Women, we earn about 90 percent of what men do until age 35. After that the number falls to between 74 percent and 82 percent. At the current pace of change, the AAUW forecasts we won't reach parity until 2119.

And it's not just our choices that are to blame. You can point a big fat finger at society.

- In 2012, a study published in the journal *Proceedings of the National Academy of Sciences* (*PNAS*) looked at what happened when equal-on-paper applicants for a position as a laboratory manager were assigned male or female names. The men were rated more competent and more hireable and given higher starting salaries and more mentoring *by more male and female evaluators.*

- In 2014, researchers at the University of Maryland asked a study group comprising more women than men to evaluate the performance of two computers on a number of factors. In reality, the computers were identical, except that one was named Julie and one was named James. When asked how much they'd pay for the computers, the study group said Julie was worth 25 percent less.

- In 2016, a study of more than 10,000 physicians affiliated with medical schools around the US compared the salaries of female docs to their male counterparts, while holding other factors—age, experience, faculty rank, specialty, research productivity, and clinical revenue—equal. The men earned an average $20,000 a year more.

- And in 2017, at the annual meeting of the American Economic Association, a panel of women unveiled new research about gender bias in economics (the dismal science is more dismal for women, apparently), including the fact that the most popular Econ 101 textbooks refer to men four times as often as women—and when women are mentioned in examples, they're more likely to be shopping or cleaning than, say, running a company.

I could go on (and on). I won't. Not earning up to your potential isn't good for anyone: you, your family, the children who watch your every move, the younger women in your orbit who do likewise, or society as a whole. Research has shown that women who do earn more are more likely to learn about our finances, take control of our finances, and be confident about the actions that we do take. (This, by the way, makes total sense. Once you have a stake in anything—whether it's cards on the blackjack table or a child on the field at a soccer game—you're more likely to be engaged in the activity and invested in the outcome.)

And for anyone who is worried about a spouse getting ruffled if you start to earn as much or more than he does, know that research from *Money* magazine showed the opposite. In households where women earn as much or more than men, spouses were happier with their relationships, "as much in love," and had better—"hotter"—sex. In fact, *Money* reported "the most satisfied partners of all were the husbands in egalitarian and female-breadwinner marriages." #justsaying

What Is "Underearning"?

As we came through the recession, you probably heard the term *underemployment*. While unemployment measures people looking for jobs who are unable to find them, underemployment measures highly skilled workers in lower paying jobs and part-time workers who'd rather be full-time.

Underearning is similar. It isn't strictly about making a low salary. It's about making less than you know you could—and being unhappy about it. If you're working in a social services job and are content with your paycheck (which is competitive for your industry but not, say, investment banker–sized) because you're doing work for the greater good, you're not an underearner. If you're living a life of voluntary simplicity, you're not an underearner. But if you're working a job—even a six-figure job—where you know you could be making more, should be making more, wish you were making more, and you aren't taking steps to remedy the situation, you're an Underearner with a capital *U*.

And you're far from alone. CPA Belinda Rosenblum, who runs the blog *Own Your Money*, recently conducted two surveys of her (mostly female) readers. She asked: "What's the biggest challenge you want to work on right now? Fifty-one percent said underearning."

Interestingly, underearning is not strictly about money. It's about the things you aren't able to do or have because of money, about not making the most of your time, about choices you regret and joy you don't experience. And it's painful. Because when you're underearning, you know it and that makes work a constant reminder that something is *wrong*. Every day, when you walk into the office or open the shop or sit down at the computer, you're on notice that you're being cheated (even if the person cheating you *is* you). Some days that feeling subsides, but others it stays with you like a migraine on the edge, and occasionally it boils over.

What makes it worse is that underearning typically isn't a one-and-done experience. It's a lifetime pattern. People who underearn have a history of underselling themselves. And it's not just an unwillingness to negotiate for an initial salary or ask for a raise (though that is a problem). If you're an employee, it's staying in a job you outgrew long ago. If you're an entrepreneur, it's setting your fees too low to begin with or not raising them frequently enough. It even shows up in excessive volunteering.

GETTING OVER THE GUILT (AND FEAR) OF GETTING MORE

To break the pattern, we have to understand it. Underearning happens because of what's going on inside of us. Sometimes this relates to low self-esteem, in our work lives and in our relationships. Other times it's an unconscious (and false) belief about how the world works.

Spiritual leader and author Marianne Williamson famously said: "Our deepest fear is not that we are inadequate. Our deepest fear is that we are powerful beyond measure." Actually, Williamson is more famous for the fact that Oprah embraced the quote and shared it with the world. But either way, it explains why so many of us don't pursue earning and amassing more.

Money—as we discussed in Part I—is many things to many people. It's security, independence, freedom. But it's also power. The more money you have, the more power you have in your relationships, your community, your workplace, your life, and the world. That's uncomfortable, particularly if you like how your relationship is going or your place among your friends or colleagues. If you were to all of a sudden have more, what would that do to the status quo? Would your spouse resent it? Would your colleagues think you were trying to leave them behind?

"Women are so deeply relational and there is that piece—the estrogen piece—that is fearful of rocking the boat, of harming relationships," says money coach Mikelann Valterra. "There's a fear of being seen by other people as, 'Boy, she thinks she's better than.'"

From a historical perspective, that fear is completely understandable. In researching her book *Prince Charming Isn't Coming*, author Barbara Stanny asked a therapist: "Why are women so afraid of their power?" And this wise therapist pointed out: "Powerful women have been burned at the stake." That's true. And even if we don't think about that very often in those stark terms, there is an understanding in our collective unconscious that over time we have been punished for speaking up, for taking up space, for assuming positions of authority, for being powerful. To this day, Stanny notes, it still feels safer to many of us "to water ourselves down so we don't make waves."

But there are other fears as well. We may worry that if we made more money, we would have to give up personal time with our family, our friends, *the gym*. Or that if we made more money, we wouldn't be able to manage it. We may fear that making more money will put us at center stage and make us more visible, which would in turn make us more vul- nerable. When a man really screws something up at work and gets nega- tive feedback, he takes it in—then generally lets it go. When a man does something amazing at work and gets a big pat on the back, he takes it in—then generally lets it go. Many women are not like that, especially when it comes to feedback of the negative kind. We're hugely impacted. We dwell. The thought that more criticism might be coming our way because—in effect—we put ourselves out and asked for it can be down- right terrifying.

Oh, and then there's this complication: these fears are typically not conscious. You have to be willing to dig a little to figure out what is hold- ing you—specifically—back. Perhaps it jumped out at you in the last few paragraphs. But if it didn't, try to take a little time and think about what it is about earning more that bothers you. Make a note of it somewhere so that you'll remember.

Not a Zero-Sum Game

That I'm a theater geek will only surprise those of you who don't follow me on Twitter or listen to my podcast. And like many theater geeks I have a deep and abiding love for Jason Robert Brown, who has written many musicals but had no real mainstream hits. (That is what happens when you write musicals like *Parade*, about the real-life trial and lynching of Leo Frank.) Brown came closest with *The Last Five Years*, which ran off- Broadway and was made into a movie with Anna Kendrick and Jeremy Jordan in 2015. It's the story of a failed marriage, based on Brown's own, and follows Jamie (a struggling writer who manages to break through) and Cathy (a struggling actor who doesn't) through the ups and downs of their relationship and careers. It tracks one forward in time and the other backward, and they meet in the middle only once, which probably doesn't help matters. But the music is fantastic.

Anyway, I laid out this whole story so that I could tell you about one particular lyric. The couple is fighting—again—about Jamie's success and Cathy's lack of it. And he sings: "I will not lose because you can't win." That is the sentiment at the heart of this problem. Jamie (and to some degree, Cathy, who wants him to be just as frustrated as she is) is just like the many women who don't understand that success is *not really a zero-sum game.*

We think that if we are more successful, then maybe we are taking something away from some other equally deserving person, maybe even from someone we know. I know that this sort of magical thinking exists because I've experienced it. After I had broken through in my work life, thanks largely to regular TV exposure, I heard from several people that a woman I used to work with—someone I once considered a pretty good friend, in fact—was complaining that I had "stolen her career." It was mind-boggling to me, because she was never interested in personal finance or even business journalism, though she did have television aspirations. But in her mind, she couldn't succeed because I had.

It's a little harder to make the same argument strictly about money because at the end of the day $1 + $1 = $2, and the company pie has to add up to 100 percent. But let me try.

Let's go back to the young woman on my staff who got the $5,000 raise. I looked at our projected revenue stream as well as the cumulative salaries of the people on my payroll, how much we were spending for office space (more than last year), and the other expenses we had incurred lately and decided I could afford to do this. I was comfortable if it meant I would earn that much less myself, but I was also pretty sure that I could do this in a way where I wouldn't.

One thing we'd started doing was having our weekly podcast transcribed so that we could create articles from the material. There were two solutions: a human transcription service at $8,000 a year and a machine one at a fraction of that. A machine transcript needs to be cleaned up, but that takes minutes, not hours. I chose the machine. Was that precisely where the raise came from? Not *precisely.* But you get the idea. Assets—including time—are malleable. We can choose to spend less to pay our employees more.

So, who lost in that calculation? I suppose you could argue the human transcriber lost. But that seems like not a very good value-for-dollar proposition in this case—a business model that isn't long for the century. Besides, I don't know that person. So, I can choose not to feel bad about that. (And if that human transcriber is a) reading this and b) smart, they'll buy some software and lower their prices to enable them to compete. In that case, their business grows and they win, too. You're welcome.)

By the way, this logic holds even if you're working in a helping profession or for a nonprofit (which, contrary to their names and reputations, often make plenty of money). In her practice, business coach Karen Southall Watts has seen that counselors, teachers, and others who see themselves as doing work for the greater good particularly hate asking to get paid what they know they deserve. "When it comes to the moment of handing over the invoice or signing the contract, their gut instinct is to [revert] to that 'I'm a helper' mind-set and offer a discount before someone asks for it." You might as well be saying: "Pay me in magic beans and kittens."

Finally, let's separate the guilt we feel at earning more individually from the guilt we feel about societal inequality. It's important to distinguish between income inequality in the country—and the huge societal problems it causes—from income inequality in our individual professions, companies, workplaces, and fields. If you feel really strongly about closing that gap, wouldn't it be better to earn more yourself and give some of the money to an organization focused on the cause or—even better—hire another woman and pay her what she's worth?

SOLVING THE PROBLEM

Like many things in life, solving this problem starts with intention. You have to recognize that you're not earning up to your potential and decide that you really want to change things. There will be several steps to this process, but that's the first one and you can't skirt it. For some people (you know who you are) change is exciting. The thought of new jobs, new people, new relationships, new *anything* lights them up with excitement. There are other people who have been buying the same toothpaste since 1973—and they are the majority.

For most people, change brings a loss of control, it brings uncertainty. When you're in a new scenario, it may take some time to get up to speed, and that period of feeling incompetent—particularly for women—is tough to abide. Change is *uncomfortable*. So we avoid change, and that holds us back. "I have been at the same company for fifteen years," says Lauren, 30s, a human resources director in New York. "I move around within the business every few years and I try to negotiate for a higher base salary [each time], but it's still nowhere near what I could get if I was negotiating externally."

There's no way around it. You're going to have to be willing to be a little uncomfortable in order to get where you're going. And you're going to have to be okay with the fact that asking for more—whether you're raising your rates or requesting a raise—may make the person on the other side of the table a little uncomfortable, too. But you may also be surprised by that person's reaction. They may be expecting you to negotiate and surprised (or even disappointed) if you don't.

I've heard this many times from my husband, who spent nearly two decades hiring editors and art directors for the Hearst Corporation. He almost always held a little something back so that he'd have it to give when the candidate started negotiating. And he would tell me how disappointed he was when the person—often a woman—didn't step up. Results from a CareerBuilder survey showed the same thing. More than half of employers are expecting and willing to negotiate—half of the candidates just don't ask.

GETTING TO YES

There are a number of tactical things you can do to help yourself (and others) through this hurdle.

First, get clear on your number. Deciding you want to earn more but not how much more is a little like deciding you're going to run a race but not settling on whether it's going to be a 5K or a half marathon. You can base that number on external factors or internal ones. Looking outside yourself means doing research (on sites like PayScale.com, Glassdoor .com, or Salary.com) on what people with your skills and experience earn. Job postings that specify what they're paying when bringing in new candidates with your skills can be similarly helpful.

Or you could—gulp—ask someone.

More women than ever (thank you, millennials) are comfortable sharing how much they earn with friends and colleagues. Meredith Rollins, the former editor of *Redbook* magazine, told a story on my podcast of how—when she was promoted to take the helm of that magazine—she sat down with the woman who would be moving into her job and coached her on just how much she should be asking for.

Mika Brzezinski talked on the podcast (you are listening to the podcast, aren't you?) about how she's negotiating *with* some of the new hires at NBC to be sure they're fairly paid. "I am personally taking them by the hand down to the front office," she says, explaining, "I know what I get paid. I know how long I've worked for it. I have insight. What you need is a voice and maybe a friend and a sense of your value." Those three things, she says, are all it takes to get the job done. I've done the same with some of the newer, younger personal finance experts on the scene—coaching how much to ask for a speech or a blog post. It feels great to pay it forward.

It also helps to have a sense of how much you're contributing to the bottom line. In early 2018, *Grey's Anatomy* star Ellen Pompeo gave an interview to the *Hollywood Reporter* in which she revealed just how hard it was for her to ask for more money. She had been told by the show's creator, Shonda Rhimes (who also spoke to the magazine), "Decide what you think you're worth and then ask for what you think you're worth. Nobody's just going to give it to you." But Pompeo worried about seeming "too greedy." Then she learned that the show where she's had top billing for fourteen years had made $3 billion for Disney. "When your face and your voice have been part of something that's generated $3 billion for one of the biggest corporations in the world, you start to feel like, 'OK, maybe I do deserve a piece of this.' " Her new $20 million contract made her the highest-paid woman on dramatic television.

The other way to approach the question of your number is internally. It's a question of not just what you need to earn but what you *want* to earn to create the life you really want. Think concretely: Not what *would* life look like if I could earn this much more. But what *will* life look like when I start earning this much more. The first is a wish. The second, an intention. And be specific about what it's for. A house in a neighborhood that would give you a shorter commute? Padding for your retirement account to ease your anxiety? A foreign trip once a year? Private school for the kids? A wardrobe upgrade? The ability to give more away? There's no right or wrong, so don't judge yourself.

That's how Robin Arzon does it. A former corporate lawyer, Arzon has over the past seven years built herself into a health and fitness brand, becoming the head coach for Peloton, which streams cycling classes into thousands of homes every day. When she's thinking about how much to charge for a business opportunity, Arzon spends some time "really just thinking about how I want to feel in my security ten or twenty years from now," she said. And once she comes up with that price? Arzon says: Add tax. "Whether you are a freelancer, entrepreneur, business owner, or stay-at-home parent, know your worth, then add tax." Tax, by the way, is not just the amount freelancers should be adding because they're going to have to pay it to the government come April (hint, hint). Tax is your innate value. It's different from the hourly price you put on your time. It's the premium for your participation, for the energy you're putting into this project, for the idea that strikes you (you know, the one you jot down in the journal you keep by your bed) in the middle of the night. It's a little something extra because when you're in, you're all in.

I've gotta say: I love that idea.

The People and the Words

In the previous section, we talked about the three cogs in the wheel of getting paid fairly—a voice, a friend, and a sense of your value. You've got the latter. Now you need the other two. The voice may be the hardest to harness. Think about how easy it is to advocate on behalf of a child who needs your help. You're doing something for someone else. It can be equally difficult to advocate for you—particularly when you're asking for money—because it feels selfish. So flip the equation. By putting, and keeping, yourself in the equation, you're doing something *for* your clients, *for* your organization.

As for the friends, there are people who propel you forward and those who hold you back. If you're surrounded by the latter, it's time to get some more supportive ones. And if you're having trouble finding them, I suggest looking among the younger women you know.

Julie, 30s, the marketing analyst from Baltimore, says that she is the one her friends come to for this sort of advice. "I'm confident in my skill set because I went the digital marketing route, which more veteran marketers are afraid of. I've gone to my employers and said, 'Give me more money or I'm going to walk.' It's worked every time—maybe not to the full extent, but a conversation is had where we come to a middle ground."

And when Jessica, 30s, a beauty marketing executive from New York, didn't have the skills, she turned to her best friend. "I really didn't know how to ask, but my best friend taught me that if you don't ask they won't give," she says. "So, I put together a deck of everything I've done to grow the company, to bring in revenue. You have to show them why you deserve more money. That's the only way to do it."

Now, I wouldn't suggest going with Julie's actual verbiage—*Give me more money* is a little harsh (insert wink emoji here). If you're stuck, try this conversational flow:

EXERCISE 6

HAVE A REVENUE-BOOSTING CONVERSATION

1. Express excitement. You can say, "I'm so looking forward to joining your team." Or, "I'm so excited about taking on this project." The idea is to start with some words that tell the other person you're jazzed. Do this in some way that implies this is or will soon be a done deal (even though it's not quite).

2. Confirm that you're the right one for the job. They already suspect this or you wouldn't be talking money, but it's a good thing to do. Say something like, "I know I'll bring just the right skill set to the team."

3. When it's a salary negotiation, cite your research and experience in asking for more. "I've done some market research, and people with my experience and expertise are earning more along the lines of X." Or, "I can't justify making a move from my current company unless it's a salary of X."

4. If you're raising your rates, emphasize how much you value your client's business and the relationship. Then, be straightforward and honest. "My rate for 2019 is going up to X."

Two more points before we wrap this puppy up. One, when you're negotiating, remember there is more than money on the table. There may be highly subsidized health insurance (valuable), a 401(k) match (valuable), stock options (valuable), and extra vacation time (priceless). Factor those into the numbers you run as you're evaluating your possibilities. And two, remember that when you're negotiating for a position with a new company, you have more leverage than you will—likely ever—have again. Searches can be lengthy and pricey. Even a small company may spend hundreds of dollars on ads, countless hours weeding through them, and even more hours on interviews. They are already invested in you because you are the one they want. What they do not want to do is go back to square one, making this the absolute best time for you to ask for what you want and get it.

That is one reason switching jobs is the best way to make more money. And it's why if you really want more money and can't get out of the cost-of-living-increase cycle, you may have to take a leap and pretend. When I was a staff writer at *Smart Money* magazine, I was in this position. I knew I was underpaid, so I went to my boss, presented my case, and asked for more. He told me his hands were tied. In order to pay me more, he was going to have to make a case against losing me to his boss. "Go get another offer," he said.

Now, I know that may not *feel* very good. You're wasting other people's time by getting them invested in and excited about you. (And if the new employer catches on to the game you played, they may have the same reaction that I've seen my husband the recruiter have. He says: "They're dead to me.") But it does work. It can produce a significant salary bump. That said, you can get away with this only once with each employer. And if your current employer doesn't come to the table with more money—which may happen if a) they don't have it or b) you're not as valued as you think you are—you may have to jump ship anyway. But it may also open your eyes to your true value in ways that surprise you. You may learn that your current skills translate to opportunities that you had no idea you were qualified to take on. And, as a result, you may decide to go anyway. More Money + A New Challenge = What Could Be Better Than That?

What Have We Learned

- *Asking for more money for you is not a cakewalk. But it does get easier—and you get better at it— with practice.*

- *The more of us who ask for more, the more normal it will become. You can't ignore the studies that show when women negotiate, managers—both male and female—are less likely to want to work with us. As negotiating becomes the norm, not the exception, this will change. After all, what are they going to do? Not hire any of us?*

- *Consider what happens if . . . This is how I finally got myself to the table. The other person can say: "That's way out of range"—at which point, you have to question if this is worth your time. They can say: "That's a little high, how about this much"—at which point the negotiation begins and you can choose to take it or leave it. They can even say: "Okay"—and if they say it too quickly, this is the point where you start kicking yourself for not asking for more. And remember Money Rule #63: If you don't ask, the answer will always be No.*

Where Do We Go from Here

At almost every HerMoney Happy Hour, I've asked the question: Are you an investor? And, despite the fact that we have 401(k)s, IRAs, 529s, and other investments in our own names, the answer is almost always no. That's a problem. In the next chapter, we step up to the investing plate.

CHAPTER 6

Yes, You Are an Investor

Here's a snippet of conversation from a HerMoney Happy Hour outside San Francisco.

JEAN: *So, how many of you would call yourselves investors?* (Of the ten women around the table, two hands go up.)

LINDSAY: *I can't take credit for being an investor. I'm just sticking my money in a SEP-IRA.*

HOPE: *I know we, as a couple, have investments. But I, personally, don't do it.*

KELLY: *Do passive investments like index funds even count as investments?*

ERICA: *I wouldn't say putting your money in an index fund means you're an investor. I don't manage my money each day. I don't manage it each year. I just put it in. I look at the statements and I hope that it's going to get the average that they say you're supposed to get. But to me, that's not an investor. An investor is someone who takes time during the day to look at stocks to see how they're doing. And, maybe when a stock is fading off, trying to time the market.*

JEAN: *That would make you a bad investor.* (Cue laughter. Fade to black.)

It's Time to Own This

Just to recap: Women are very clear about what we want from our money. We want to satisfy our needs for safety and security. We want to increase the time and freedom we have to pursue the things we want to do and offload those we don't. We want choices in career, education, community. We want control. We want to pay it forward. And, yes, we want nice stuff—there is absolutely nothing wrong with nice stuff.

There are two ways to produce the resources we need to check off all those boxes. We can earn money by working and saving. And we can earn money while we sleep by putting our savings to work—in other words, by investing.

Working is wonderful, but you can't do it forever. Saving alone was fine in the 1970s and 1980s, when you could park your money in a bank account and it would earn high single or even double digits. Today, however, you're lucky if you get a sad 1 to 2 percent, which means you are losing money after taxes and inflation. Even as interest rates rise, the amount you'll get paid on your savings has a long way to go before it will actually make you money—that's why keeping more money in the bank than you need to satisfy your short-term and emergency needs may *feel* safe, but isn't.

Investing is the way to stay ahead. That means using the money you've set aside for the long term (generally five-plus years) and using it to buy a mix of stocks and bonds (and maybe some other assets like real estate) that makes sense for someone your age who is expecting to retire when you are and has a similar approach to taking risk.

And here's the thing: You may not *identify* as an investor even though *you already are one*. You may feel like Sara, 30s, who works in higher education in Baltimore. She says, "I'm putting my 6 percent away in my 403(b), but when it comes to investing I have no idea." And not only are you an investor, you are probably a pretty good one.

But first, let's answer some questions.

- ❏ Do you have money in a retirement plan like a 401(k) or 403(b) or an IRA?
- ❏ Do you own stock in the company you work for?
- ❏ Are you putting money into a 529 college savings account?
- ❏ Do you have an account with a brokerage firm or a robo-advisor?
- ❏ Do you have an app on your phone that saves up your spare change and invests it?

Check any of those boxes and you are an investor. You just don't feel like one. Research shows most women don't. So, let's clear up the difference between investors and what Erica described as people *"who take time during the day to look at stocks to see how they're doing. . . . And, maybe . . . [try] to time the market."* Those people are traders. They buy and sell much more frequently, betting their investments will fall in price as well as rise (a practice called "selling short").

Investing is slower, longer term. It is a process with which you can and should be patient. And—although traders and investors sometimes use complicated, technical tools and analysis to tell them what to buy, what to sell, and when—investing does not have to be that complicated in order to set you up nicely for the future.

Boring Is Better

In researching this book, I heard a consistent desire from women to get smart about investing.

- *I just wish I was more knowledgeable about the best things to do with my investments in order to get the greatest return.* (Julie, 30s, Pennsylvania)

- *I'm pretty confident in mortgages, insurance, being a consumer, credit cards, savings accounts, checking accounts. What am I insecure about? I'd like to understand investments so that I have control over how well my money performs.* (Natasha, 30s, New Jersey)

- *I'm very confident in my ability to make money, budget, and save money. [Not] investing it. There are so many areas that are so complex when you get down the rabbit hole. I feel a little overwhelmed.* (Michelle, 30s, California)

Everybody: *Breathe.*

There are three things that determine how successful most investors are.

1. The amount you save. Generally, you want to put away 15 percent of whatever you're earning for the long term. Women are already better at this than men.
2. Asset allocation or the mix of investments—stocks (the riskiest ones), bonds (a little less risky) and cash (safe, except for the taxes/inflation thing)—you choose to balance risk and reward.
3. Security selection—the particular stocks, bonds, or funds you choose to put in those asset buckets.

Number 1 is the most important. Number 2 a close second. Number 3 you hardly have to think about at all. In fact, I'm not even going to go into how to pick a stock or bond. You want that? Read a different book. And here's why:

Number 1: The Amount You Save. Say you have $100. You invest it and over fifty years it grows and becomes $1,000. The first $100 was your original principal—or how much you saved. The other $900 was your return. Now, some people would make the argument that that $900 was totally dependent on where you chose to invest that money, in other words the mix of assets you put it in. But, if you didn't have the $100 to begin with, there would have been nothing to grow. As Alexandra Taussig, senior vice president of Women and Investing, Analytics, Marketing and Communications at Fidelity, explains: "Just like everybody knows you can't out-exercise a bad diet," you can't asset allocate your way out of a savings problem. Saving is first and it is nonnegotiable.

So, how much *do* you have to save? A solid 15 percent of whatever it is you're earning—year in and year out—should get you to the point where you can retire knowing you'll have about 85 percent of your pre-retirement income (including what you'll get from Social Security) and that it will last about thirty years.

You will know if you're on track if you line up with guidelines that investment companies have developed to help steer you in the right direction. These are Fidelity's: By age 30, you should have 1x your annual income saved for retirement. By 40, 3x. By 50, 6x. By 60, 8x and by retirement, 10x.

Right about now, you're having one of two reactions. You're nodding along or you've got iced coffee coming out of your nose. I know this because in late 2017, I tweeted out these benchmarks and Twitter went nuts. So nuts that the *Washington Post* wrote about my tweet. I got thousands of likes, but also well over a thousand comments—many of them snarky. Here's how it went down.

> Jean Chatzky
> @Jean Chatzky
> By the time you're 30, aim to have 1x your annual income set aside for retirement. At 40, 3x; at 50, 6x; at 60, 8x; and by retirement, 10x.

Responses included:

> Good advice. On a related note, does anyone know any handy recipes for leftover unicorn?

and

> But how much avocado toast are we allowed?

Look, I get it. If you aren't close to those guidelines yet, they seem impossible. But what I'm telling you is that if you can get to saving that 15 percent—including matching dollars you might be receiving from your employer—you'll hit the marks. And if you're not there yet? Don't aim to get there all at once. Increasing your rate of saving by 1–2 percent every six months to a year is a better way to go.

Moving on to **Number 2: Asset Allocation**. There is so much research on the importance of asset allocation and how it compares to the importance of security selection (picking stocks and bonds) that diving into it will make your head spin. Here's all you need to know: In 1986, three researchers did a deep dive into the performance of pension plans (which are broad pools of retirement assets) and determined asset allocation was responsible for about 94 percent of the performance. In other words, it wasn't about the individual investments. It was about the mix. The paper they published is still cited to this day. There have been follow-up studies since then. Some say asset allocation accounts for 80 percent of performance, others 100 percent, others a little less. But in every case it's the lion's share.

That's pretty good, right? So why do individual investors bother picking stocks at all? Because they want to *win*. If you've ever watched financial news, you've heard the word *benchmark*. A benchmark is a standard we use for comparison. In the world of chocolate chip cookies, a benchmark might be the Toll House. It works because pretty much everyone knows what Toll House cookies look like, taste like, even how to make them. So, you and they can judge: Is your recipe better, worse, or just as good?

In the world of investments, benchmarks are indexes that have been created to represent big pieces of the overall market. The Dow Jones Industrial Average and the S&P 500 are two popular stock benchmarks. There are others for bonds, and others for mutual funds. The whole point of security selection or picking individual stocks, bonds, or mutual funds is to try to *beat benchmarks*.

What if you decided that you didn't care about that? What if you decided that the benchmarks—and since its inception, the Dow has gone up a little less than 8 percent annually, the S&P 500 10 percent—were just fine? Congratulations. You have just given yourself permission to be a boring investor.

That means finding a way to pick an asset allocation that works for you (I've got you covered on that, keep reading). Just as importantly, though, you've just made a decision about what you're not going to do. You're not going to *meddle*. Once you flesh out your asset allocations, you have to let them do their work. The markets have a bad day? Week? Month? Turn off the television.

Many studies show women are better investors than men. The primary reason for this is that we do not meddle. We don't trade as frequently, which means we don't have to pay the cost to trade. But frequent trading also leads to mistakes; you have to figure out not only when to get into an investment but when to get out. Who needs to worry about this? Not me—I am a very boring investor. And I'm guessing not you, either.

What's Holding You Back?

And if all of that information still isn't enough to get you feeling good and calm and comfortable? You have to do it anyway. Have to because you are going to *need the money*. As we've already discussed, we still make about 20 cents on the dollar less than men. We still are the ones who dip in and out of the workforce to care for kids and older parents. As a result—even though we save a greater percentage of our earnings in our 401(k) and other retirement plans—the average balances in our plans are about 50 percent less than that of men, according to Vanguard. Investing can help close the gap.

So let's line up the obstacles standing in our way and move past them.

KNOCKING DOWN OUR INVESTMENT OBSTACLES

Obstacle #1: You don't want to do something you don't understand.

Anna, 50s, the lawyer from Philly, is sitting on a lot of cash from her divorce. "It's in a savings account and I have no idea what to do with it," she says. "I'm nervous so I'm stuck." As a woman who likes to know the answer to every question before I ask it, I get that. Recently, though, I've gotten hooked on *The Great British Baking Show*, which airs on PBS and Netflix. If you've never seen it, it's a master class in doughs and sponges, proofing and pastry cream, and the show has me experimenting with yeast breads and strange flours. Some of my concoctions haven't risen much and others have been fairly ugly. They've all been edible. And I've learned that the only way I'm going to get better and more confident at this is by doing it.

Investing is a little like that. Doing it *helps you* understand it. Once you open an investment account, you know how to open an investment account. Once you transfer some money into that account and put it to work by, say, purchasing an S&P 500 Index fund or a target-date retirement fund (more on those in a moment)—you know how to buy an investment. (If you've got a plan at work, just enroll. The steps will flow seamlessly.) Then sign up to make regular monthly contributions into that same investment, register for online access, and start checking it. You'll start to see the ups and downs in the portfolio. Because you're regularly adding to the investment, you'll see more ups than downs, which is good for your confidence. And you'll start to feel like you get it. You may also find you know more than you thought you did. When women and men have been given multiple-choice quizzes to test their financial knowledge, scores are pretty equal once you remove the "don't know" option, which women elect far more often than men.

Obstacle #2: You don't want to lose money.

More than half of women worry about that, according to a 2015 Merrill Lynch report. Other women don't like the feeling of a competition—particularly one they're sure they're going to lose. "It feels like someone always loses in the stock market," says Jess, 30s, a freelance graphic designer in Chicago. "That's how I feel about sports. All that investing stuff seems like a lot of people trying to get a leg up on each other, and it doesn't feel good to me." Trading is that kind of competition. Investing is not. In investing, everyone *can* get a trophy. And given sufficient time—no one has to lose. History bears that out. If you invested your money in the S&P 500 over the *worst* thirty-year period in history, you would still have made about 8 percent a year.

Obstacle #3: You think investing is the same as gambling.

It's not and here's why: When you're gambling, you are wagering your money on a particular outcome. If that outcome doesn't pan out—your lottery numbers aren't called—you lose it all. When you're investing, you're *buying* something—a piece of a company when you buy a stock, small pieces of many when you buy a mutual fund—and that something has *value*. Over time, that value can go up or down, but by not buying just one stock, but instead spreading out your risk by buying many (what we call diversification) and by investing over time, you are vastly increasing your chances of making money, not losing it.

Obstacle #4: You don't trust the financial industry.

Why would you? asks Fidelity's Alexandra Taussig. "This industry has been created for men, by men." It has given us Ivan Boesky. Michael Milken. Gordon Gekko (okay, he's fictional). But Bernie Madoff isn't. The financial industry often doesn't sound like us— much of the language used in the products is very male. It doesn't look like us—only about one-quarter of financial advisors are women. But, in fact, the financial industry is not the least trustworthy one in the US, according to a 2017 study. It's third. Oil and petroleum is number 1. Yet, just like you wouldn't let lack of trust stop you from filling up your car, you don't have to trust the financial industry to take advantage of it. You have to shop smart and find a single firm or individual that you want to work with. And if you'd prefer to work with a woman, today you have choices. Abdicating for lack of trust should not be one of them.

Finally, even once the obstacles are cleared, you may need a little shove to get going. I suggest finding your why. Why do you need your money to grow? To stop working? To put your kids through college? To give more to causes you believe in? While men are often focused on accumulating as much as possible—#winning—women are more motivated by our life goals. Making investing personally meaningful can help propel you to take the steps you need (yes, *need*) to take.

The Buckets

I said I wasn't going to go into how to pick a stock or bond—and I'm not. But putting your money to work does involve making two choices. First, you choose the right type of account for your needs. Then you choose the investments to put in those accounts.

Think of accounts as buckets that hold your investments. There are three basic types of buckets:

- **Taxable:** Includes plain vanilla bank and brokerage accounts. You generally[6] pay taxes on proceeds you realize each year.

- **Tax-deferred:** The government wants to incentivize you to save more for these goals and so you get a tax deduction for making a contribution, and you don't pay taxes on the money while it's in the account. When you withdraw it at retirement (which you can do starting

☞ There are some investments that have preferred tax treatment attached to them as well—like municipal bonds. The government does this to make them more attractive as well.

at age 59½ and must do starting at age 70½), you pay
income taxes at your current rate. These include: 401(k)s,
403(b)s, and other workplace retirement plans, and
traditional IRAs.

- **Tax-free:** You've already paid taxes on the income you
  put in, but the money grows without taxes being paid and
  you can withdraw it tax-free. These include Roth IRAs
  and health savings accounts (HSAs) as long as you use the
  money for health expenses.

In general, we want to put as much of our money into tax-deferred or
tax-free buckets as possible. We also want to grab any other incentives
or freebies (like matching dollars) that are available. Then we move on
to taxable accounts.

So, if you have a retirement plan at work, the rough order of accounts
you'd contribute to would be: 401(k) or other workplace plan, HSA, Roth
or traditional IRA (eligibility depends on income but you can do this in
addition to a workplace plan), taxable account, 529.

If you're an employee but don't have a plan at work, the order would
be: traditional or Roth IRA, HSA, taxable account, 529. How do you
decide if you want Roth or traditional? (Or, if you're in a workplace plan,
when you want the 401(k) option?) Look at taxes and flexibility. If you
think your tax bracket is higher now than it will be in retirement, a traditional IRA makes sense. If you think your tax rate will be higher later
(generally true for younger people) or that all US tax rates will be higher
later, a Roth makes sense. Many people (including me) have money in
both Roth and traditional IRAs. We're hedging our bets on the uncertainty of both our own and the country's future tax rates. A Roth is also
more flexible in that you can withdraw your contributions (though not
the earnings) at any time without penalty—so you can get at the money
if you need it. You can also let it grow forever and pass it on to your kids
if you want.

If you're self-employed and can surpass the annual limits on traditional IRA and Roth contributions (currently $6,000 plus another $1,000 for people 50 and over), you'll want to start with a SEP-IRA or a solo 401(k), followed by the other accounts—HSA, taxable account, 529. SEPs are best for individuals or people who work just with a spouse. They allow you to sock away up to 25 percent of your W-2 earnings or 20 percent of your net self-employment income—and get a tax deduction for doing so. The hitch is that if you have other employees, you have to contribute the same percentage of their salaries that you do of your own. A solo or individual 401(k) is only available if you have no employees. It comes with more paperwork, but may allow you to contribute more money. And, unlike with SEPs, you can borrow from your 401(k).

The Filling

Once you've got your buckets, you can begin filling them up. Here are five ways to go about it in the order of the effort they require, from practically none to more substantial.

Strategy 1: Do it for me—Target-date fund

What is it? A fund of other mutual funds designed to help you retire at a particular date (you'll recognize these by the date in the title). It invests your money more aggressively when you're younger and less aggressively when you're closer to retirement and needing to use it. For example, Vanguard's Target Retirement 2050 Fund has about 90 percent of its assets in stocks now. But by 2050 it will have a little less than 50 percent, and five years later closer to 34 percent. Many work-based plans will automatically put your money into the target-date fund that they think is right for you unless you elect to do something else.

How to use it? You pick one with a date that lines up with your projected retirement, and then—and this is important—you put all of your investments in this one fund. If you put some of your money in a target-date fund and some in other, say, stock funds, it defeats the purpose of keeping your risk in line with your retirement.

How much are they? The average target-date fund charges an expense ratio (or fee) of about 0.75 percent annually.

Strategy 2: Robo-advisor

What is it? A computer-driven financial planning service. You answer questions about your age, financial situation, goals for retirement, and attitude toward risk. The computer uses your answers to figure out an asset allocation for you and then keeps you in balance over time. Many also offer tax-loss harvesting, which is a way of minimizing capital gains taxes (a good thing).

How to use it? You open an account with a robo-advising firm (the biggest are Wealthfront and Betterment; Ellevest is aimed at women) and start contributing. Big firms like Schwab, Fidelity, Vanguard, and others now also offer robo-advising services. The pure robo start-ups aren't typically able to manage your 401(k), but you can open IRAs, SEPs, and taxable brokerage accounts with these firms.

How much are they? Fees range between 0.2 percent and 0.5 percent of your portfolio annually.

Strategy 3: Managed account for your workplace plan

What is it? A way of bringing more personalized advice to 401(k)s and other work-based accounts. You fill out a questionnaire about your goals, and a robo-advisor (or, sometimes, a person) selects the appropriate asset mix for your needs and then keeps the portfolio in line with your goals. Managed accounts also offer advice on how much to save, how long to work, and other information that can be helpful in amassing enough for retirement.

How to use it? Talk to your retirement plan provider at work about whether these services are available, then follow their lead.

How much are they? Fees range from free to more than 0.5 percent of your portfolio.

Strategy 4: Financial advisor

What is it? A person, either independent or within your brokerage firm, that you hire to manage (or help you manage) your investments based on your goals.

How to use it? That depends on you—and the advisor you'll choose. But you'll find much more on how to find and work with an advisor coming later in the chapter.

How much are they? Generally 1 percent to 2 percent of your portfolio annually, though some charge by the hour, others by the plan.

Strategy 5: DIY

What is it? A portfolio that you build yourself and then rebalance once or twice a year. This is the most labor-intensive solution on the list, but even this doesn't have to be difficult.

How to do it? You open an account and then regularly invest in a mix of assets that works for your age and risk tolerance. New York–based financial advisor Stacy Francis specializes in working with women. She helped us develop these portfolio recommendations. Note: You can satisfy them all by just buying index funds—funds run by computers that track a particular portion of the market. (Where the recommendation says "Short-Term Bond," for example, you'd buy a short-term bond index fund.) Index funds are both inexpensive and, because the investments in the portfolio don't change all that frequently, tax-efficient. (FYI: exchange traded funds, or ETFs, are index funds that trade like stocks. They'll work, too. Active traders often prefer ETFs because they're cheaper.)

IF YOU'RE IN YOUR 30S		
Asset Class	Asset Subclass	Target
Bonds	Intermediate-Term Bond	13.0%
Bonds	Short-Term Bond	8.0%
Non-US Stocks	Emerging-Markets Equity Fund	15.0%
Non-US Stocks	Int'l Developed Equity Blend Fund	19.0%
US Stocks	US Large Cap Growth	20.0%
US Stocks	US Large Cap Value	20.0%
US Stocks	US Small Cap Blend	5.0%

IF YOU'RE IN YOUR 40S		
Asset Class	Asset Subclass	Target
Bonds	Intermediate-Term Bond	18.5%
Bonds	Short-Term Bond	11.0%
Non-US Stocks	Emerging-Markets Equity Fund	13.5%
Non-US Stocks	Int'l Developed Equity Blend Fund	16.5%
US Stocks	US Large Cap Growth	18.0%
US Stocks	US Large Cap Value	18.0%
US Stocks	US Small Cap Blend	4.5%

IF YOU'RE IN YOUR 50S		
Asset Class	Asset Subclass	Target
Bonds	Intermediate-Term Bond	25.0%
Bonds	Short-Term Bond	13.5%
Non-US Stocks	Emerging-Markets Equity Fund	12.5%
Non-US Stocks	Int'l Developed Equity Blend Fund	14.5%
US Stocks	US Large Cap Growth	15.5%
US Stocks	US Large Cap Value	15.5%
US Stocks	US Small Cap Blend	3.5%

IF YOU'RE IN YOUR 60S AND GETTING READY TO RETIRE		
Asset Class	Asset Subclass	Target
Bonds	Intermediate-Term Bond	42.5%
Bonds	Short-Term Bond	19.5%
Non-US Stocks	Emerging-Markets Equity Fund	8.0%
Non-US Stocks	Int'l Developed Equity Blend Fund	9.0%
US Stocks	US Large Cap Growth	10.0%
US Stocks	US Large Cap Value	10.0%
US Stocks	US Small Cap Blend	1.0%

How much does it cost to invest this way? It varies dramatically based on the cost of the investments you select for your portfolio. If you choose index funds, however, it can be less than 0.2 percent of your portfolio annually. (It should be cheaper, BTW. You're doing all the work.) In 2018, Fidelity introduced two funds that cost zero.

Automate

No matter which way you choose to fill your portfolio, there is one thing you *must, must, must* do for your sanity and your future security. You have to automate. This means setting up a system to make regular contributions into your account and your mix of assets—without you having to think about it even a little bit. The magic of 401(k)s is that they do this via paycheck deduction. But if you don't have that option, you can still set up a system with your brokerage firm or financial advisor to move money automatically on the same day each month into the account and assets of your choice. Then all you have to do—all you *get* to do, I should say, because this part is a pleasure—is watch it add up.

Making the Money Last as Long as You Do

The biggest financial fear women have is running out of money before we run out of time. It's not unreasonable considering the fact that we live five years longer than men and still earn far less. But today we have tools, solutions, investments, and insurance policies that we can use to make this whole question of running out of money a nonissue. Then we can go back to worrying about more important things, like whether our go-to brand of chicken stock has added sugar and if Aruba or Antigua is better for winter break.

Traditional pensions provided guaranteed income—a lifetime paycheck of sorts. Those of you who work as teachers or in government, belong to a union, or have served in the military may still have this. With the exception of Social Security, which is a sort of pension but not one ever intended to cover our full cost of living, the rest of us are out of luck. So we have to stitch together a paycheck of our own. How?

Putting Together Your Retirement Paycheck

Be strategic about Social Security.

It's possible to claim your benefits as early as age 62, but for every year you delay claiming until age 70, your monthly benefit will grow another 8 percent a year, a guaranteed return that's tough to beat anywhere else. The math here is a little complicated, but if you're single, you have to live to age 80 for the bigger checks you'll receive each month to make up for the years of smaller checks you missed. If you don't think you'll live until 80, you should claim sooner. Couples are more complicated and one of you may want to begin benefits sooner. I suggest paying a few bucks to run a Social Security calculator like the one at SocialSecuritySolutions .com or MaximizeMySocialSecurity.com, where a computer will tell you precisely the best claiming strategy for you.

Consider annuities.

Annuities have a bad reputation for being complicated (sometimes true) and laden with fees (they can be). But if you choose the right ones (the simpler, the better), they can be a good option for providing another income stream. I prefer fixed annuities—both immediate ones and deferred (also called longevity) ones. Buying a fixed immediate annuity is like buying a paycheck. You pay a premium now and receive a monthly payment for a set number of years or for life. A deferred or longevity annuity is similar except that you pay the premium now and don't start the payments until some point in the future. That allows the annuity company to hold on to your money for a while and grow it, so deferred annuities are less expensive than immediate ones.

In addition to the financial benefits of annuities, there's a psychological component to purchasing one—the income is guaranteed. I'm a fan of making sure you have enough arriving each month in the form of paychecks from Social Security and annuities or other pensions to cover predictable fixed costs like housing, transportation, food, and healthcare. Think of it like sleep insurance. You may not have enough for fabulous extras, but you know you don't have to worry about the basics at all.

Withdraw strategically.

For years, the standard advice for retirees has been to withdraw no more than 4 percent a year from your retirement stash. In real life, however, withdrawals have varied. Morningstar researcher David Blanchett has noted that retirement withdrawals—when graphed—resemble a smile. They're heftier in the early or *go-go* years of retirement, when we travel a little more, spend more on entertainment and eating out, and finish up the mortgage or college payments. They tail off in the middle or *slow-go* years, as we stay home more and the kids are out of school and (hopefully) out of the house. And they pick up again in the later or *no-go* years as healthcare costs begin to add up. JPMorgan Chase research confirmed these findings and noted that retirees are surprisingly willing to roll with the punches of the markets. When their portfolios are performing particularly well, they withdraw a little more. When the markets are down and their portfolios lagging, they withdraw a little less. It often works out to the difference between one and two vacations a year.

But the 4 percent rule remains a good starting place (though if the markets are down in your early retirement years, consider taking a little less). Just as important as how much you withdraw is the order in which you make withdrawals. Earlier in the chapter we talked about how you have taxable, tax-deferred, and tax-free buckets. The standard advice has been to withdraw from the taxable accounts first and allow those assets that are growing without being taxed to continue to add up. But those tax-deferred assets are not allowed to grow forever. You're allowed to start withdrawing from 401(k)s and IRAs at age 59½, but you *must* start withdrawing from them by age 70½—and the size of your withdrawal is based upon your age and the balance in the account. By waiting, you may end up being forced to make bigger withdrawals at age 70½ and you may end up owing more taxes overall. I know. It sounds like it's getting complicated. And it is—which is why as you're transitioning to retirement, working with a financial advisor is a must in my book.

Finding Help You Can Trust

You have undoubtedly become aware through the reading of this book—if you didn't know it before—that I am a big fan of financial advisors. I have an advisor, my mother has an advisor, and I often recommend advisors to others—particularly at points of life transition.

A number of studies have tried to quantify the value of advice—the amount, after the cost of the advisor, it adds to your returns. Most of this research (from Envestnet, Vanguard, Merrill Lynch, and others) puts the value at about 3 percent a year. Morningstar estimates it's half that or 1.5 percent a year. Still, even that—over years—is significant. If you invest $500 a month for 30 years at a 6.5 percent return, you'd end up with about $550,000. At an 8 percent return, you'd have $750,000. And at 9.5 percent? $1,025,000.

And you can't attribute all the value of having an advisor to investment returns, which to some degree are out of your (or the advisor's) control. Your advisor might tell you to increase your savings rate, restructure the way you're paying down your debts, help you strategize to avoid taxes. All of those provide a quantifiable return.

Finding one you feel you can trust, however, can be complicated. Most advisors in the US are men. When they're hired to work with couples, it isn't unusual for most of the communication to be directed to the man—who is assumed to be in charge. The result is an interaction that can be uncomfortable, verging on disrespectful.

"I make the money and my husband manages the money," says Claudia, 60s, from Philadelphia. "For the most part things are fine. But every once in a while I get panicked—mostly because I feel like we're taking on too much risk—and I tell him I want to see the financial advisor." That's the right impulse. But the interaction always disappoints her. Claudia asks her questions. The advisor answers them in a way that she doesn't really understand—"he throws a bunch of numbers at me"—and then she goes away for a year or two until she gets worried again and the scenario repeats itself.

I asked why she stays with him, and she replied: "That's the thing. I picked somebody else and my husband picked this guy. But because my husband is taking care of the money, I let him have the guy he liked. There's some relationship there. Some bond. I sort of feel like I exclude myself. Maybe they sit there and talk about football. I doubt it's about my money."

I told Claudia the same thing I would tell every one of you in that scenario. That financial advisor may be the best stock picker in the universe. He is not the right financial advisor for her.

Keep in mind: Your advisors want something from you. They want your business. They want the privilege and profit that comes from managing or helping you manage your money. They want you to recommend them to your friends. If you feel like Claudia, steel your nerve and fire that advisor. (This is not that hard. If you've already found a new advisor, they can initiate and handle the transfer of assets for you.) Or, like a significant other (or a puppy) with potential, *train* them to be the advisor you want them to be. Tell them what you're missing (clearer answers, more prompt return calls, a detailed plan) and see if they can conform to meet your needs. But understand: you are the customer.

When you're ready to find an advisor, start with word of mouth. Ask colleagues and friends with financial lives like yours if they have someone to recommend. (The benefit to colleagues is that you'll meet advisors already familiar with the minutiae of your company's retirement plan.) If nothing turns up, you can turn to the Internet. The Financial Planning Association (plannersearch.org), National Association of Personal Financial Advisors (NAPFA.org, for fee-only planners), and Garrett Planning Network (GarrettPlanningNetwork.com, for fee-only planners who work hourly) all have search engines that allow you to find planners nearby. Do a quick background check on anyone you're considering at BrokerCheck.FINRA.org (the Financial Industry Regulatory Authority). I also like to see that people have their CFP®, or Certified Financial Planner™, designation. Then schedule three or four consultations. They should be free.

At your meeting you'll want to ask:

- *How will we work together?*
- *What's the division of labor?* What will the advisor do versus what will you do yourself?
- *How much will this cost me each year?* This gives you a way to compare advisors who charge in different ways (some charge fees for the plan or hourly rates, others a percentage of the assets they manage for you).
- *What do you do when the market takes a really bad turn? Communicate* is the right answer. In most cases, the right advice is going to be "stick to the plan," but some hand-holding during these periods is part of the job.
- *Are you a fiduciary?* A fiduciary is someone who pledges to act in your best interest (rather than their own) at all times. A no-brainer.
- *Can I have references and see a sample plan?* There should be no problem with this at all.
- *And . . . anything else that's on your mind.* If you have a special needs child/are in your family business/are determined to take a year off and travel around the world, you'll want to ascertain they've worked successfully with other clients in similar situations.

Even more important than the questions you ask are two other things that should play a big role in your decision. First, what did the advisor ask you and how well did they listen? This relationship isn't about the advisor and you, it's about you and the advisor. You come first. There should be a flurry of questions about your goals in life—because the job of an advisor is to help you achieve them financially. If the conversation is one-sided and you're doing all the listening, that's a very bad sign. And second, how did you feel in the room? Comfortable? Able to ask all your questions? Like maybe you could have coffee with this person? All good signs. Intimidated? Reluctant to speak up? Stupid? *Next.*

What Have We Learned

- *If you've got money in a retirement account, a brokerage account, or an index fund, you are an investor—you may just not be a very engaged one. That has to change if you want to make the most of your money for tomorrow.*

- *Investing is really only a matter of picking the right account to put your money in, then the right mix of investments to put into it. You can do this yourself or you can get some help. Either way, it doesn't have to be difficult or expensive.*

- *Accumulating the money you need to meet your goals is the first half of the equation; making the money last as long as you do is the second half. You need a strategy for this as well.*

- *There may come a point when you want to hire a financial advisor to give your financial life a once-over or just make sure you're on track. Finding one to meet your needs is a matter of asking the right questions.*

Where Do We Go from Here

Today, many women are investing in ourselves by building our own businesses.

This gives us a means of controlling both our money and our lives—but only if we do it right. Whether you're aiming at launching a full-time enterprise or a side hustle, the next chapter has the 411.

CHAPTER 7

Investing in Your Own Thing

*I was commuting past the Oakland, California, airport
every day [to my job at a solar power company] while raising
my kids. That takes an hour with no traffic, and those days
didn't exist. But I did very well. I became the regional head
of my company. And I was miserable. I didn't like being in a
company where I was constantly on a treadmill. I also saw an
unserved need in the marketplace—the market for solar power
was opening up, solar and power storage was growing, and I
knew that if big corporate buyers could buy [from a women-
owned business] they would.*

*So, two years ago, I gave up that huge salary and bonus and
started my own company with a partner. We do advisory work
to bring in current cash and we're developing large-scale solar
batteries [large enough to power 35,000 homes or more], which
is a growing field. What we brought in this year is nothing like
what we made from our former employer. But over the years I
know I've made companies a lot of money. Ultimately, I feel I'll
be more financially successful on my own.*

—*Dana, 50s, entrepreneur*

∽

On that day in 2016 when Dana hung out her shingle, she was just
one of the 887 women launching a business *every single day* according to
the *State of Women-Owned Businesses Report* from American Express.

More than 9.4 million businesses—30 percent of US businesses—are women owned. But because the rate at which women are opening business is climbing at 1.5 times the national average, that percentage is growing fast.

I was another one of those founders, though I came to the party earlier—in 2005—and for a completely different reason: I got fired. I had been at *Money* magazine for almost a decade when it happened. The editor who had hired me had been kicked upstairs, I'd applied for the top job (which I didn't get), and the new guy wanted to put his stamp on the place. But this time was different. It was happening *to me*. And I was petrified.

I went through my contacts and made a few calls to folks I knew at other business magazines. But it very quickly became clear that replicating my salary with the office and the assistant, the 401(k) and the bonus was going to be difficult, if not impossible. So I asked myself: What if I didn't take another full-time job and instead cobbled together a string of part-time and freelance ones? In what was a harbinger of the gig economy to come, I was already doing a lot of work on the side—writing columns and books, giving speeches. What if I just did more of that?

"Start a company," my accountant said as he handed me the phone number for a service that would—for a few hundred bucks—help me incorporate over the phone. I dialed the number so quickly, I didn't even have an answer when the customer service rep asked me what this new venture would be called. Photos of my kids nearby inspired me to borrow—and string together—their middle names. "Samuel Bennett, Inc," I said. (In later years, a colleague who was asked too many times to explain the name spun a yarn about how *Mr. Bennett* was a patriot and pioneer in finance from the time of Alexander Hamilton. I've told it myself on occasion.)

I opened a business checking account, applied for a corporate credit card to more easily track expenses, bought health insurance, and hired an assistant. I decided to forgo office space. My assistant was happy working from her apartment. I was *not* really happy working from home

(I was lonely) but I didn't feel like paying for an office. I dealt with the lack of colleagues by trying to see at least one real person a day. (Usually it was my friend Diane for a morning run.) And a decade later, my small business is less small—and growing. We have space in a WeWork coworking space, a diverse workload that includes a weekly podcast, the HerMoney.com website and newsletter, *Your $*—an in-school magazine that goes to two million fourth, fifth, and sixth graders, and some consulting. Today, if some company offered me the equivalent of the job I was fired from, I wouldn't think twice about turning it down.

WANT VS. NEED, REDUX

When you listen to the stories of women who start businesses, the reasons they strike out on their own seem almost as varied as the businesses themselves. In fact, they can be boiled down to two—want and need. Either you want to start a business because you sense an opening in the marketplace, or you need to start one because your other options pale by comparison.

In the business journals, the two groups are called "opportunity" and "necessity" entrepreneurs.

Necessity entrepreneurs tend to be a little less aspirational, a 2017 report from Stanford University explains. They want to control their own lives and destinies but aren't generally out to make a fortune. Many want to take care of their families and need more flexibility to do that. Some even see an ageist society staring them in the face and jump before they're pushed. They want a comfortable lifestyle, but they're fed up with having to look for cover if they have to dash out the door before the boss.

Opportunity entrepreneurs think bigger. They see that—after investing their start-up capital—they can earn more money by going it alone. They are more likely to hire other people. They create faster-growing businesses. And they do so by spotting an opportunity—an unserved or underserved niche in the marketplace—and going after it.

That can be exceedingly profitable, as entrepreneur Jennifer Hyman learned. Hyman's younger sister, then 25, had been invited to a wedding. She went to a department store, selected a trendy designer number, and put it on her credit card without a second thought. As the older, more responsible sibling, Hyman thought this was ridiculous. "I was nagging her," she told me on the *HerMoney* podcast. "I really tried to get her to wear something she already owned. And her response to me was that she didn't want to wear something in her closet because she had been photographed in everything in her closet—and those photographs were up on Facebook." (Instagram, where those photos would more likely show up today, hadn't even been invented.)

For Hyman, it was "a lightbulb moment." She realized that young women of her sister's generation didn't really care about the *owning* aspect of many things. They were comfortable subscribing to a service like Netflix for movies or Spotify for music. When they needed a ride, they called an Uber or Lyft; it didn't matter that they didn't own a car. And when it came to their clothes, owning didn't matter nearly as much as being able to walk into a room feeling confident, knowing they weren't going to get dissed on social media for being an outfit repeater.[7]

☞ Just for the record, this is an area where there is a huge generational divide. Like my favorite fictional female sleuth Kinsey Millhone—whose creator, Sue Grafton, sadly passed away in 2017 with one book left to pen in her alphabet-inspired series— I'm a great believer in the all-purpose black dress. Unlike Millhone, I have more than one, but I've repeated at weddings, funerals, and yes, on TV. My 21-year-old gluten-free, dairy-free daughter would sooner chow down on a massive bowl of fettuccini Alfredo.)

By now, I'm sure you know where I'm going with this. In 2009, Hyman and her partner Jennifer Fleiss launched Rent the Runway, which rents single items for special events and has a subscription program where you can rotate everyday items through your closet four at a time. The company has over 1,000 employees, millions of members, and by the end of 2017 had raised nearly $190 million in venture funding. Hyman is the CEO.

A Business or a Hobby? A Freelancer or an Entrepreneur?

Maybe you've had it, too—that lightbulb moment. Maybe you're one of those people who have what you're sure are brilliant business ideas on a regular basis. JJ Ramberg, the host of the weekly small-business show *Your Business* on MSNBC, explains the all-too-typical trajectory: "You're sitting around with your partner or your spouse or your kids and you say, 'I have this idea!' Everyone gets excited about it and tells you it's great and [as a result you're convinced that] it's great. And you spend all this time and money on it and you launch it and *nobody* wants it."

There are a lot of fantasies we have about starting our own businesses. One of the most dangerous is the Mrs. Field's Fantasy. It goes something like this: *I make the best/most beautiful/most unusual toffee/ succulent gardens/personalized dog paintings anyone has ever seen. If I quit my day job and focused on that, I'd be a gazillionaire.* The problem is the many assumptions within that singular daydream. Is your toffee indeed the best, or is it just the best in your family or your small town? Will people worldwide want to buy succulent gardens not just tomorrow and next year but for the foreseeable future? If you did quit your day job, how many dog paintings would you have to create to match your current salary (much less achieve gazillionaire status), and could you do that with just your two hands?

And—this is important—would you continue to enjoy something that you do for pleasure if you had to do it for work? One of the most common fallacies in starting one's own business is that because you like doing a thing, you'll be good at running a business that does that thing. But running a business is about so much more than making the widget or providing the service.

Say you're an Etsy seller—not too big a leap as 88 percent of Etsy sellers are women—and your thing is making knitted Minnesota Vikings hats. Every winter, there's a surge in orders as people decide one of your creations would make the perfect holiday gift for their tough-to-please brother-in-law. Now imagine that this year the Vikings are the odds-on favorite to win the Super Bowl. Orders are rising fast. How would you scale to meet that? Would you want to scale to meet that? Are you ready to hire other knitters or invest in (gasp) knitting machines, to oversee quality control, to deal with the fact that more customers overall may mean more dissatisfied ones? Do you want to do all this? Or do you just want to create your fabulous hats and make some extra money?

If the Vikings/knitting analogy leaves you dry, there are hundreds of other ways to ask this question. Do you want to open a restaurant—which requires getting permits, requisitioning supplies, advertising, and marketing—or do you just want to cook? Do you want to put your fabulous style on display by opening a cutting-edge boutique—which requires ordering, invoicing, staffing—or do you want to find some way to earn money from your fabulous style sense, perhaps by being a stylist or personal shopper?

In other words: Is this a business or a hobby (or a side gig, which is somewhere in between)? If it is a business, is it the sort you can grow or one that just enables you to make a nice living working for yourself? They are not the same thing. If you work for yourself and can find a few sustainable clients, you can build a nice, generally stable lifestyle. Building a very large company is something entirely different. So is building a small or midsize company, for that matter.

If you don't believe me, just look at payroll. As a business owner, payroll has been a huge frustration for me. It's time consuming if you do it yourself, expensive if you hire out, and even if you do hire out, you have to be constantly watching over your shoulder for mistakes. There's a terrifying statistic that one out of three businesses currently does payroll wrong—which means you could be in for costly fines. And payroll is just one tiny little example of all the things that go into the business soup.

By the way, there are no right or wrong answers to this question of scaling versus freelancing, business versus hobby. The mistake, says Marc Prosser, cofounder of FitSmallBusiness.com, is not understanding

a) the difference and b) that you have to choose. In his practice, Prosser sees people who are conflicted. "They're either upset that their business isn't growing or they're upset about the lifestyle," he says. "You can have a great lifestyle basically taking on select clients. Or you can try to build a large business. But the two don't work together."

Is Being a Business Owner in Your DNA?

There are certain characteristics that many successful entrepreneurs have.

Trait #1: You're obsessed (in a good way).

Is it hard for you to get to lunchtime, let alone through the day, without thinking about your idea? Does building this thing—whatever it is—get your heart beating a little faster? If you're motivated not by financial gain, not by freedom, but by making sure this enterprise exists in the world, you're what Susan Oleari, Chicago regional president for BMO Private Bank (who has funded many entrepreneurs over her career), calls a "passionate creator" and have a great shot at both business longevity and business success.

Trait #2: You're a (calculated) risk taker.

But also a substantial one. Diving into a business of your own may entail quitting your job (risk), investing your savings (risk), hiring others (risk), and raising capital (risk). Not everybody is suited for that. If you're unsure, examine the downside.

Before she launched her solar venture, Dana, 50s, from California, took a look at what would happen if the business failed. "I knew that my kids' college was set and that the worst thing I would have to do was downsize," she says. "I was perfectly prepared to do that."

Trait #3: You're up for working all the time.

If you're someone who starts work at nine, finishes at six, and always takes the same lunch hour, launching a business (at least the sort you want to grow) may not be for you. Christin, 30s, from Seattle, says, "What scares me is that it becomes almost an obsession. You have to pour yourself into the company, and I wouldn't want that to affect my relationship with my husband or take too much time away from my family." She's got a point. A new business is not unlike a new puppy—what you put in is what you get out. Even those entrepreneurs who are seeking more autonomy—like Dana—often put in long days. "I probably work sixty hours a week—but before the schedule was not mine," she says. "I never had much control."

It's important to note this start-up schedule doesn't have to last forever. Six months after launching the daily newsletter *The Skimm*, founders Carly Zakin and Danielle Weisberg took back control of their calendars and started scheduling things like exercise, seeing friends and family, and time *off* e-mail. They realized the company wouldn't be sustainable if they weren't healthy enough to run it, so they figured out a way to make it happen. More than five years into their successful venture, they still operate this way.

Trait #4: You're willing to admit what you don't know.

One of the most important things an entrepreneur does is acknowledge what they don't know—and be willing to either learn it or surround themselves with people who do, or a combination of the two. I've hired consultants to fill gaps in my full-time roster, particularly helping me get up to speed with social media strategy because technology is not my strong suit. Which is not to say entrepreneurs shouldn't have an ego—they should—egos go hand-in-hand with confidence. But confident people also have the ability to say, "I don't know," and understand it isn't a death sentence.

Trait #5: You solicit feedback and adjust.

Kathryn Minshew, founder and CEO of job and career site TheMuse.com, credits this—above all—with her success. (And she *is* successful—the Muse now employs 120 people and in 2017 raised $20 million in venture funding.) "I became laser focused on where the criticism and where the kudos were coming from," she told me on the podcast. "We had thousands of people at the beginning using the site and they would write in and say, 'I love this. I have never found anything like this product.' Or, they would be angry at us and they would say, 'Here are five things you could do to make the site better.' That, by the way, is great feedback. Because if somebody cares enough to tell you what you could be doing better, especially if it's things that you want or are planning to do, that's a sign that you're onto a need that they're essentially encouraging you to solve."

PROOF OF CONCEPT

After the idea phase for many businesses but before you invest tremendous resources, it helps to prove it will work.

That means research. Before launching Rent the Runway, Jennifer Hyman did a deep dive into the economics of the average closet. She knew that the average American buys sixty-four items of clothing every single year—regardless of how much they earn. She also knew that 50 percent of the items in our closets have been worn three times or fewer, and that that percentage has been climbing over the past decade. That confirmed her hypothesis that we want constant newness and constant variety. She also knew that because 70 percent of Americans are projected to live in cities by 2030, closet space was going to be increasingly tougher to come by. Put it all together and you can see how Hyman came to believe that "the closet of the future" is going to be one where everyone will have a subscription for getting dressed.

There are many ways to gather the sort of information you need to build a business case. Say you want to open a bakery (a longtime fantasy of mine). You might start, small business expert Marc Prosser suggests, by spending a day at each of the local bakeries in your area, pretending to be a customer. By counting the people coming through the doors and watching what they're buying, you'll be able to figure out how much revenue the bakeries are taking in. You can learn an awful lot just sitting in parking lots and watching, but you may find you don't need to be that stealth. "People are often surprised at how open other business owners are to sharing their experiences," Prosser notes.

All of that information you're gathering becomes the backbone of your business plan. For the record, Hyman and her partner Jennifer Fleiss—who met at Harvard Business School—wrote one. Many other entrepreneurs don't.

For three years, I hosted a daily one-hour radio show on Sirius XM's Oprah and Friends channel. I interviewed countless entrepreneurs and in the process of eliciting their stories always asked two questions: How much money did you launch with? And did you have a business plan? The answer to the first was almost always "$5,000." (Even Spanx founder Sara Blakely started her billion-dollar journey with that.) The answer to the second was almost always no.

So, I am mixed on the necessity of a formal, formatted business plan that checks all the business school boxes. I am not mixed on knowing the answers to the following basic questions that every business plan should pose:

- What need is this business satisfying?
- How are we different from the other solutions in the market?
- Who are our customers?
- How will we reach them?
- How big is our market, how fast is it growing, and why?
- How will we make money?
- What are the economics of our business: How will we get from pricing to break even to profitability? What kind of money will we have to spend to get there? And how long will it take?
- What does our competition look like?
- Who will do all this work?
- Are there any legal or regulatory hurdles on the horizon?

You don't just have to know the answers, by the way, you have to know the answers *in detail*. You may have decided that the best way to reach your customers is online, so you're planning to advertise on Facebook or Google. That's a start, but you have to go further. If you give yourself a $10,000 marketing budget, you need to know how many people you're going to be able to reach with that. Marc Prosser explains: "It's only once you dive deep enough to understand that it costs, roughly, $3 a click on Google in your industry and you know how many of those clicks actually become customers, you can figure out that you're going to have to pay $300 a customer. All of a sudden your assumption that you'll get customers for $50 doesn't work."

You don't have to do all of this yourself, by the way. There is a wealth of free business mentoring advice available to people who look for it via the country's Small Business Development Centers (part of the Small Business Administration and searchable at SBA.gov), SCORE.org, and Women's Business Centers in general (searchable at AWBC.org).

What may happen in the process of answering these questions is that you decide the business isn't viable or that it isn't right for you—the market you thought was there isn't there, you don't have the skills or the capital to launch, or it's going to involve more tech time than people time and you're a people person. That's incredibly valuable information to have, and the fact that you've gotten it *before* you quit your job or invested thousands of dollars is huge. It's like the recent college grad who decided to work a couple of years as a paralegal before applying to law school and *hated* that work. Sure, she invested some time, but not three full years while incurring over $100,000 in graduate school debt. I'd say she won.

Where to Get the Money

Starting a business takes capital. Sometimes a little, sometimes a lot, but you need to know both how much and where it's going to come from. It will probably come as no surprise to you that women tend to rely more on ourselves for start-up funds than men do, the same way we rely more on ourselves to drive the carpool, do the laundry, and hit the grocery store even when we've already got a packed day of work. Self-funding makes sense in many situations, but not all. It's important to understand that there are other options. And even though it's more difficult for women than men to access those options, that doesn't mean that you shouldn't a) consider them and b) try them if appropriate.

According to Investopedia, the number one reason businesses fail is lack of capital, i.e., not having enough money to keep the doors open. Almost 50 percent of founders blame this when they shut down. Yet the number wouldn't be nearly this high if entrepreneurs were a little more rational—and planned—about how long it takes to be able to pay yourself a salary, let alone hit profitability.

How long it will take for your business to start making money depends completely on the type of business you're starting. If you're leaving a law firm to start your own practice—and you know your current clients will follow—you can make money from the start. Those types of businesses—where what you're selling is you and you can often keep costs down by working from home at least at the start—are easier to launch, but generally capped in terms of the amount of money that's possible to earn. If you're trying to start the next Rue La La? It's way too optimistic to figure you'll be able to draw a salary six months from now. Two years is more typical. Which is why having at least a year's worth of living expenses banked (maybe two) before quitting your day job is the way to go.

Lacking that, you can follow the path of Twitter, Craigslist, Houzz, Khan Academy, and many other businesses that were launched as side hustles. You keep your job and your paycheck, do whatever you must during the day to keep your employer satisfied, and work on your project nights and weekends. The money you need to fund your launch can come from your current cash flow or other alternatives you can access yourself. Proving that your idea has legs while you're still drawing a salary may also give you the confidence you need to take it on full-time.

It's a bit of a dance. You don't want to spend more than you have to. But you also don't want to starve your new business of oxygen by not giving it enough money to grow. That's why you see entrepreneurs turn to their savings, retirement accounts, home equity, credit cards, small business loans, friends, and family.

But wait, you ask (sounding a little too much like an infomercial): Isn't there free grant money available to start businesses? Yes and no. The Small Business Administration's SBIR (Small Business Innovation Research) program does give grants of up to $1 million. But they're largely limited to high-tech companies with great commercial potential and they're, as you might expect, extremely competitive. There are some state-run grant programs and community ones as well (and you can easily seek them out online), but most grants are very small and not all fields have them. In addition, small business loans aren't readily available until you've had your doors open for a couple of years. And getting a line of credit from a bank—even on your home, in some cases— can be equally tough. To come up with start-up capital, you're going to have to rely on you or the people closest to you. (And think twice about the latter. Sitting in a restaurant with your aunt who gave you a $25,000 business loan can be highly uncomfortable. You suspect she's wondering how you can afford to order the paella when you haven't paid her back a cent. You're probably right.) Here are the other options.

Your retirement accounts

Do I want to see you borrow money from your 401(k) to start a business? No. Do women do it every day? Absolutely. So, let's talk tactics. If you're still working for the employer where your 401(k) is housed, you can take a loan from the plan with no taxes and penalties. That's much better than withdrawing money outright, which will result in an income tax bill plus a 10 percent penalty if you're not 59½ or older. Generally, 401(k) loans are repaid on a five-year timetable at reasonable interest rates where you're actually paying interest to you. But there is a cost: While the money is out of the plan, it's not growing. And, if you leave your job, you have to pay back the money inside of sixty days or it will be treated as a withdrawal.

If you've got IRAs instead of 401(k)s, long-term borrowing is not an option. (You can roll over an IRA and access money for sixty days, but if you haven't repaid it in that window, it'll be taxed and penalized as a withdrawal.) If you've got a Roth IRA on which you've already paid taxes, you can withdraw contributions to the account at any time without penalties (the exception being money you converted from a traditional IRA to a Roth—even though you already paid taxes, there's a 10 percent penalty if you pull the money out in less than five years). If you withdraw earnings before age 59½, you'll face a 10 percent penalty.

And before all of you who are 59½ start having a party because you can withdraw money without penalty, think about what happens if your business fails. How would you replace that retirement security?

Your home

Taking out a home equity loan or refinancing your mortgage and pulling out cash simultaneously has a different set of risks. As with a 401(k) loan, treating your home as a piggy bank can be a relatively inexpensive source of capital as long as interest rates stay low (although thanks to the 2017 tax law, the interest paid on home loans used for anything other than fixing up your home is no longer deductible). But, if your business doesn't do well, you've added thousands—and maybe years—to your mortgage and you still have to pay that money back. And, if property values fall (which, as we saw in 2007, can happen), you can end up owing more on your property than it's worth.

Your credit cards

According to a 2017 Bank of America US Trust survey of high-net-worth small businesses, 37 percent of millennials—and about half that many founders of all ages—use credit cards to fund their businesses. Where credit cards are concerned, there are pros (frequent flier miles and other rewards points, zero percent financing that can last a year or more, ease) and cons (interest rates that zoom to 15 percent or higher after the zero percent teaser rate is up, ease). The cards you'll qualify for and the interest rates you pay, particularly in the beginning, will depend on your personal credit history as your business doesn't have one. So, keep your credit score up by checking off all the boxes: pay your bills on time every time, don't close cards you aren't using or apply for ones you don't need, try to keep your utilization (the percentage of debt you're using compared to your credit lines) between 10 and 30 percent on all cards individually and your portfolio of cards combined. This last factor will likely be harder to maintain if you're funding a business with plastic, but asking for increases in your credit lines before you spend heavily can help.

A personal loan

These are granted based on your personal credit score and your income (if you're planning to quit your job to start your business, apply for this in advance). They're typically unsecured, like credit cards, which means they don't require collateral. If you're unable to repay the lender, no one will take your business like they'd take your house in a foreclosure or your car in a repossession. But your credit will suffer. The interest rates on personal loans are typically higher than collateralized loans like mortgages (the fact that the lender can come after your house makes it less risky for the lender) but lower than the APRs on credit cards. Banks, credit unions, and online lenders (like Lending Club and SoFi) make loans like these. Shop around.

A microloan

These are very small loans (averaging about $13,000 according to the Small Business Administration) made to businesses, generally at low interest rates. They're aimed at helping new ventures get off the ground, and some are specifically for women. The SBA has a microloan program. Other prominent microlenders include Accion and Opportunity Fund, and many states have start-up programs. Google your state and the words *microloan* and *women* to find them.

Crowdfunding

Over the past decade, crowdfunding has become a nearly $10 billion industry, growth helped significantly by the passage of the JOBS Act, which cleared the way for "equity" crowdfunding which allows companies to seek investments this way.

Today you can look to use not only traditional platforms like Kickstarter, GoFundMe, and Indiegogo, where you might give people who donate a small reward for contributing, but also specific equity platforms like Crowdfunder, EarlyShares, and Wefunder, where people who invest get a piece of the company.

Women are more successful crowdfunders than men, according to PwC. The surprising advantage? We craft our pitches more emotionally and inclusively, and that gives us an edge. Still, most crowdfunding campaigns fail. So, if you're going to go this route, you again need to be strategic. Alex Daly, author of *The Crowdsourceress* (she got the nickname by running so many successful campaigns), explains that the *crowd* in *crowdfunding* is the most important part. If you launch this thing and nobody's there to donate, "it's going to flatline in a second," she told me on the podcast. A mailing list, strong social media, or anything else that can bring that built-in audience of people invested in the work you do to the campaign is key. And you need to be engaging with them constantly.

If you want to raise money this way, you'll need to create a company profile that tells your story briefly but well, introduces your team, highlights your plans for growth, and includes an investment profile that details how much you're raising and what funders get for their money. You'll also want to create a short video that tells your story in a straightforward, clear, and emotionally appealing way. It has to say what your project/company is and why it's important and relevant *right now* in the first thirty seconds. And you have to put yourself front and center. "They have to fall a little bit in love with *you*, too," Daly says.

Bank Loans and Venture Funding

Until 1988, women could not access capital in our own names. You might have had a profitable business with great credit, and you still would have needed a male cosigner—age sixteen or older (yes, pimply male teenagers full of raging hormones and sometimes uncontrollable impulses were considered more responsible than adult women)—before a bank would give you a commercial loan. President Reagan put the kibosh on this.

So, you can now sign your own application for a bank loan. But that doesn't mean you're going to get it. A report from the Urban Institute shows women receive just 16 percent of conventional small business (SBA) loans each year. It also doesn't mean that you're going to get enough. A 2017 analysis of customers from loan portal Fundera shows women apply for loans that are $35,000 smaller on average (including SBA loans) than the ones men apply for, are charged higher interest rates, and receive the loans for a shorter term.

Ironically, we often see applying for less in funding as a form of minimizing the risk we're taking in our businesses. But by underfunding—some say *underfinancing*—we're actually putting the entire enterprise in jeopardy. It's better to seek enough to give you the runway to make it to profitability.

Once you've got a couple of years of consistent revenues, bank loans, including SBA loans, are in range. And that's a good place to start. SBA loans are granted by banks, credit unions, and online lenders, but they're guaranteed by the Small Business Administration. That guarantee allows lenders to grant them at lower interest rates because they're not shouldering 100 percent of the risk. You can borrow up to $5 million in an SBA loan (although the average loan amount is closer to $400,000). If this sounds appealing, go to SBA.gov and start gathering the paperwork.

Because of their attractive rates, SBA loans are not always easy to get. Institutions (big banks, community banks, credit unions, online lenders) also make other—non-SBA-backed—small business loans (or small business lines of credit—which you draw upon as needed to finance day-to-day operations, only paying interest on what you've borrowed). Their rates are just typically higher, so again, shop around. And don't forget credit unions: When small business capital essentially dried up in the aftermath of the financial crisis, credit unions were still out there making loans. They often have very competitive rates. And, if you think you can't borrow from one just because you don't belong to one, you're wrong. You can join one as you borrow from it.

And then there's venture capital. If you've got a really, *really* big business idea, raising venture capital is a road you will eventually consider. It has to be really, *really* big, because VCs are not interested in your stable business that's growing 10 percent a year. VCs are looking to make one hundred times their money. And when they make a bet, they're betting on you as much as on the business itself.

What they don't often do is bet on women. In 2016, just 17 percent of global venture funding went to companies with at least one female founder, according to Pitchbook. Less than 3 percent of venture capital goes to companies with a female CEO. The Muse's Kathryn Minshew is famous, or rather *infamous*, in the VC community not for being one of those female CEOs who successfully raised money—but for the number of times she was turned down before she got it: 148. What holds women back is bias in the industry. Men (it has been documented) are evaluated on their potential, women on their track record. When you're starting a company, that track record doesn't exist. What got Minshew through was persistence—and the ability to learn from each consecutive session about what to do differently.

Her advice: Learn as much as you can about the specific investor you're pitching. "Some want you to start immediately [talking about] growth and traction," she says. "Others are looking for the story of how it came to be." You also have to approach networking as part of the process. When she was just starting out, Minshew didn't know many people in the tech community. So she started showing up at local events, introducing herself to the other entrepreneurs in her community. "They could make introductions to investors," she said. "[That's better] than trying to be the eighth person in line to corner the investor at some happy hour event." And, she advises, know what you're best at—and sell that. "There are five things that any investor might care about. It's better to be a ten out of ten on one dimension than a seven out of ten on all of them." So, is it the cool technology you've built and patent protected? Is there a huge opportunity? Is it your team? Your revenue? User growth? As she pitched (and pitched and pitched) for her seed financing round, Minshew focused on the latter. "We did our best to make that so standout that eventually people had to pay attention to us," she says.

What Have We Learned

- *There are two reasons we start businesses—we want to or we need to. It's important to understand your rationale for going into any new venture and, even if you don't write a business plan, to know the answers to questions about how and why you're likely to succeed.*

- *Getting funding for businesses in the first few years of existence is more likely to rely on personal sources—your credit, your home equity—or people you know, via crowdfunding. Tread carefully.*

- *Once you have a track record of a couple of years, you may be able to apply for and get a bank loan. If you're on a faster trajectory, raising venture funding becomes a possibility.*

Where Do We Go from Here

Buying a home is high on the list of the security that many women covet. It's exceedingly possible (and being done more than ever by single women), but you should approach it as thoughtfully as any other investment. That's even more true if what you want to buy is a second home. And if HGTV has you thinking you might want to flip (not flop), well, that's possible, too.

~

CHAPTER 8

Buying Real Estate You Live In...
and Real Estate You Don't

I am writing this chapter on a cold and quiet Saturday morning in early March. Yesterday, we had a nor'easter—some said a "bomb cyclone," which is essentially a winter hurricane—with 60-mile-an-hour winds and a mix of snow, rain, and everything in between. Sometime between the time I went to sleep last night and 6:03 a.m., when the dog nudged me this morning, the power went out and the generator went on. I slept through it all. Got up. Made coffee. Flipped open the laptop. And slid into my comfy chair.

I am content because I am home.

When I knew that my first marriage was going to end, I went house hunting. I had decided that I would be the one to move. Our family house was too big and intimidating for me to manage on my own. Besides, it didn't seem fair to fight for it; my former husband loved it—and the land it sat on—much more than I did.

I could have, probably should have, rented something. This was the beginning of 2005 and the real estate bubble was fully inflated. Bidding wars raged. Properties came on the market only to be snapped up a day or two later. No doubt, renting would have been the smart financial move. But I was determined that when my kids were with me they would be equally as at home—in rooms of their own—as they would be when they were with their dad. And in my mind (which, granted, was not functioning at its highest level) that was as much about the house as anything else.

What I wanted was very specific: It had to be in the same school district. It should not be a financial stretch. And it had to be cozy. I was taken with the work of architect Sarah Susanka, who in 1998 published a book called *The Not So Big House*, and I was obsessed with the (sadly) short-lived *Cottage Living* magazine. Both featured little Cotswolds and Capes and Arts and Crafts places with hidden nooks and crannies in which you could curl up and read a book. I could manage something like that.

What I bought—as I said: 2005—was a three-bedroom postmodern colonial with a garish marble slab fireplace and soaring ceilings. It had its pluses. The fact that it was in a gated community took snow removal and lawn care off my list. And the neighbors, as I'd eventually learn, were great. But in the moment it felt cavernous, generic, and prefab.

I turned to Susanka's website and, on her list of resources, found a decorator/contractor team (a wife and husband, actually) in the town next door and hired them with a specific budget but a not-so-specific single instruction: cozy it up. And over the next couple of months—working together—we did. A too-deep garage became a functional mud-room with drawers and hooks to hide the chaos. Built-in cubbies—and nooks—took shape in the family room. We chose a couch for seating on one side of the kitchen table. And my bedroom became an oasis loosely modeled after Diane Keaton's in *Something's Gotta Give*. (Because in 2005, who *didn't* want Diane Keaton's bedroom in *Something's Gotta Give*?)

Along the way, I discovered my own taste. To my surprise, it was more streamlined than fussy. More midcentury modern than country French. I liked art, it turned out, that had elements of words. And I pre-ferred to organize books by color (don't judge). Both my kids are out of the house now and—though I miss them—it still doesn't seem too big. I am happy when I am home.

Which doesn't mean that I am going to make money on this place, and not just because I overpaid initially. When I sell it—after you fac-tor in the cost of those initial renovations plus the later finishing of the basement, the new roof two years ago, and (oh, yes) that $9,000 generator—I will at best break even. That doesn't mean I'm sorry I bought it. I am not. But it does open the door to this discussion about buying real estate that you live in and real estate that you don't.

The Home in Which You Live

For many years, we were told our home would be our *biggest* investment. That was largely true—our parents and grandparents didn't have 401(k)s and other retirement accounts. And because home prices rose an average 6.4 percent a year from 1968 to 2004 (nationally, there were no years during that time in which prices fell), homes were also many people's *best* investment. We could feel good—brilliant!—about putting our hard-earned money into them.

Then housing prices started to flatten and, in 2007, the bubble popped. Over the next four years, home prices fell by more than 30 percent, and we started to question whether a home was an asset or a liability. Did owning it add to your wealth or, because prices couldn't be counted on to appreciate *and* you had to keep plowing money into the place, did it drain it?

The answer to that question changes dramatically with where you live. For every Brooklyn hipster who made millions by sticking it out in a once-desolate neighborhood now dotted by brewpubs, there's a family in Las Vegas or Fort Lauderdale or Kenosha, Wisconsin, where prices still are 15 to 20 percent below their prerecession peak. And there are many people who are somewhere in between.

Which is why my answer to the asset or liability question is: neither. A primary residence—and the mortgage you're paying off—is, for most people, forced savings.

The Internet is full of calculators that will tell you whether to rent or buy. These calculators are built on the assumption that if renting is cheaper than a monthly mortgage payment, you'll take the money you're saving by renting and invest it.

Have the people who designed these calculators ever met other humans? Seriously, you and I both know that any overflow of dollars has a better shot at winding up on the balance sheet of Bloomingdale's than your brokerage house.

What you get when you pay down a mortgage is a chunk of money that you can use to a) roll into the next place you live or b) fund some other later-in-life goal. (Note: You'll find more about financing at the end of this chapter.) And because humans are really bad savers unless we find some way to force ourselves to do it, this is incredibly valuable.

Sure, there will be times in your life when buying doesn't make sense. If you're not planning to live somewhere for at least five years, rent. If you're moving from your forever home to a different state or community, road test by renting until you are sure you like it. And if you have another need for the money, and renting is cheaper, it makes sense as well.

Shortly after adopting her son, Kathleen, 40s, who works in advertising, sold her Brooklyn place, pocketing a large sum of money before she moved to the suburbs. She would like to buy a house and is, she says, "always looking," but is holding off. "Being a single mother, truly a single mother, there is no ex-husband," she says, "it really is 100 percent my financial responsibility to have a lot more in cash."

Dan Egan, director of behavioral finance and education for Betterment, would agree, particularly if buying a home means there's no room left to fund the retirement account. "Women are much more likely to take a lot of the money they've saved up and put it into a down payment on a house, compared to an equivalent single male," he explains. "It's tough to say that's a bad decision, but when you put your money into one house, it's a form of concentrated investment, one with high costs and high tax consequences."

Noted. But if you can do both—save for retirement and pay down a mortgage—I'm a believer in buying. Smart buying. Which means a house in which you can afford not just the mortgage, insurance, and property taxes, but the 1–2 percent a year Harvard estimates you'll spend on maintenance, the cost of furniture, utilities, as well as lawn care and any other upkeep you plan on outsourcing. As financial advisor Kristin Sullivan points out, the bigger the house, the bigger the plans for what you'll do in the house. "You're not just doing it for an investment, you're doing it for enjoyment. So, realize that for what it is," she says. "If you're going to buy a bigger house because you love to entertain, realize that all your other expenses will increase as well. Your whole footprint gets bigger. And then it's hard to pull back if you haven't saved enough for retirement."

And then—and I know this is a little radical—I want you to think about paying off that loan *before* you retire. Some people will argue with this. They will tell you that mortgage money is cheap, largely tax-deductible money (which it has been, although interest rates are rising). They will say if you borrow money from your home at, say, 4 percent (about 3 percent after taxes) and invest it in the markets, where you earn, say, 8 percent (about 6 percent after taxes), you're up by 3 percent. You have money you wouldn't have otherwise. To which I say: I will sleep better knowing that, in retirement, when my income is likely falling, not rising, I own my house and no one can take it away from me.

As for the mortgage interest tax deduction: The 2017 tax law cut the amount of mortgage debt on which interest is deductible to $750,000 (or $375,000 if you're married, filing separately). If you bought your home before December 14, 2017, you're grandfathered in at the earlier $1 million level. (And in case you were wondering about the previously deductible $100,000 in home equity loan debt, the IRS has indicated it still is as long as you use the money to improve your home and not, say, pay off credit card bills.) Is it a valuable deduction? Sure. But it still means you have debt. As Hawaiian real estate developer Abe Lee explains, "If you have a dollar in interest payments and you get a 35 percent tax deduction, you still have to pay 65 cents in interest. You still owe money."

BUYING A SECOND/VACATION HOME

Buying a second home is a little like having a second child. You don't even know you want one—in fact, you may still feel as if you're on shaky legs when it comes to doing all the right things with your first—when you wake up one day and you're just ready. And because you've experienced all of the firsts with house number one—first middle-of-the-night roof leak, first buyer's remorse when the paint now covering your entire first floor turns out to be more lavender than gray, first moment of panic when someone (hopefully not you) backs into the garage door—you're excited to do it over. You're excited to do it *better*.

And you may very well jump in the water. But before you do, it's important to understand that second homes are different. And not just because you can no longer deduct mortgage interest (though properties you already own are grandfathered). "I own a second home in the mountains and it's the worst investment I've ever made," says financial advisor Kristin Sullivan. My husband often says that aside from marrying me (I hope you're rolling your eyes—I certainly am), the house we bought on the Jersey Shore was his best. The truth is likely somewhere in the middle.

There are four main reasons you may be thinking about buying a second home.

1. You want a space of your own in a place you go frequently.
2. You're picking a place to snowbird or eventually retire full-time.
3. You see an opportunity to make money through rental income or appreciation.
4. You are Oprah and have not two homes, but approximately seventeen, and each one is not a single home but a compound.

Let's take Oprah off the list and run the scenarios down for the other three.

Reason 1: You want a space of your own in a place you go frequently.

Almost ten years ago now, my husband and I bought a second home in a place called Long Beach Island, New Jersey. From May to early

September, we use our house every weekend and spend several full weeks as well. During the colder months, we're there sporadically—if at all. By February each year, my husband often remarks: "I forget we even have a house." Kristin Sullivan works the opposite side of the calendar. She uses her mountain house primarily for skiing. "Let's be generous," she says. "Let's say I spend fifteen weekends a year there and then it sits empty the rest of the time."

Whether it's a winter house or a summer house, the bills are year-round. You have to pay the mortgage, HOA dues, utilities, cable, *whatever*. There's also the cost of paying someone to keep an eye on your place (the average vacation homeowner lives 200 miles away, according to the National Association of Realtors) when you're not there. Even if you buy a place for $100,000 and sell it for $300,000, you have to figure all of those expenses into it before you can calculate how much you've really made. But while prices have been rising on average in recent years, there's no guarantee of appreciation.

The average purchase price for a second home in 2016 was $200,000, according to the NAR. Beaches are the most popular location, followed by lakefronts, then the country. In 2016, for example, though vacation home prices rose an average 4.2 percent nationally, in the tony Hamptons area of Long Island, they fell by more than 7 percent. And when the economy does turn down, vacation home prices drop faster and further than those on primary homes. This makes sense. If money gets tight while you're trying to pay mortgages on two houses and one is the place in which you live most of the time, you're going to eliminate the second.

Another issue that vacation homeowners who don't rent their places out sometimes face is guilt. When you have a vacation place, it can make it difficult to justify paying to go elsewhere. "Having experienced all this, I really discourage people from owning vacation homes," Sullivan says. "I'm all about seasonal rental instead. That costs a mere fraction of owning a vacation home and gives you flexibility."

And yet, also having experienced all this, I have to say I'm the complete opposite. It's true we don't vacation elsewhere in the summer, but we don't mind. The best advice is to try to figure out if you're going to be like Sullivan or like me *before* you buy. And long-term rentals are the answer for that. Before we bought in LBI, we rented for four consecutive Augusts to be sure we could handle everything from the 2½ to 4 hour drive—depending a) on how honest we're being and b) on traffic—to the lack of things like a big grocery store or movie theater to the overall laid-back feeling of the place. We wanted to be sure our kids were comfortable there as well, and that our friends and family would visit. Only afterward did we pull the trigger.

Reason 2: You're picking a place to snowbird or retire full-time.

I am now at the age where the word *Florida* is coming up in conversations more than it used to. Not Florida as in "we're surprising our kids with a trip to Disney." But Florida as in "we were down visiting our parents and decided to look at real estate ourselves." Depending on where you live and work, Florida may be Arizona or California or the Carolinas or somewhere else, but the thought is the same. You're starting to think seriously about the next phase of your life, but wondering if it might be smart to dip into the real estate market now.

It can be. Buying a retirement place before you retire has financial benefits. It's easier to qualify for a mortgage while you're still working; you also get a head start on paying that mortgage down or even off. You'll have time to settle into the place without having to live there full-time, which gives you the opportunity to both figure out if any changes or renovations are needed and make those changes while you're not underfoot. And you'll be able to assess what living there will cost you— again, while you're still working, giving you the opportunity to try to speed up or slow down the retirement clock until you're sure you have enough.

Road testing a second house you plan to use for these purposes is even more important than road testing a house you plan to vacation in. And it should be a lengthy road test—a few months is much better than a few weeks, and a few days is, for all practical purposes, useless. If it still feels like a vacation (i.e., you've experienced neither rain nor boredom) you haven't stayed long enough. I know too many stories of people who up and retired to Tucson (or wherever) only to find that the people weren't *their* people and the food wasn't *their* food. Keep in mind, this is no longer just about finding a place you can relax regularly and often. It's about access to good medical care, a range of services (grocery delivery may not be something you need today, but down the road it may come in handy), culture and entertainment, and transportation.

The other important consideration with this purchase: size. You may envision this new oasis as the place where your kids and, eventually, grandkids will come to visit, and then start looking for enough bedrooms to house them all simultaneously. Be realistic. Will everyone actually spend time there together? Or will they dip in and out? And is it really worth buying a bigger house you have to furnish, heat or cool, and maintain year-round for a week or two every other year? Or would a couple of nights in a hotel with meals in your house be just fine?

Reason 3: You see an opportunity to make money through rental income or appreciation.

With the rise of sites like Airbnb, HomeAway, and VRBO, making some extra cash by renting out your vacation place has never been easier. But that doesn't mean it's easy. There are tax laws to consider and here's how they work.

If you rent your house for only fourteen days or fewer, you can pocket the money (there's no limit on what you can charge) without reporting it as rental income on your tax return. If you rent your house for more than fourteen days, it becomes a business for tax purposes. How that business is treated by the IRS depends on how much time you use it yourself. If you use it for only fourteen days (or 10 percent of the time it's rented) yourself, you can deduct rental expenses and up to $25,000 in losses each year. If you use it for *more* than fourteen days (or 10 percent of the time it's rented), you can deduct rental expenses but not losses.

And, if those fourteen days don't seem like enough, note that any time you spend fixing up or maintaining your property doesn't count. Home-owners have been known to capitalize on that.

And there are other complications. You'll reap the most money by renting at peak times on the calendar—which may be exactly when you want to use it. Zoning is another big consideration. Are short-term rentals allowed in your town or by your homeowners' association? Do you need a business permit? Are you required to collect sales tax? Keeping the place rented means scouring the market to stay on top of competitive pricing, making sure it's clean and in order before the next renters move in, being responsive to e-mail queries, and dealing with problems as they arise.

In effect, you either devote a big chunk of your time to managing this property or hire someone to do it for you. Just a note of caution, says Denise Supplee, founder of SparkRental.com, a company specializing in automating the rental process for landlords, and a former property man-ager herself. "Short-term rentals are especially tough," she says. "They require a lot of work."

Buying Investment Property . . . to Flip

Let's play a game. I'll throw some names at you and you see what pops into your mind.

- Joanna Gaines
- Drew Scott
- Christina El Moussa

If what you're seeing are people with picture-perfect hair sitting in picture-perfect homes, congratulations: you're an HGTV devotee. (If you're seeing shiplap, you may even be addicted.)

And you are not the only one. In 2012, the network was the sixteenth most popular cable channel. For the month of July in 2016, it was first—without a doubt one of the reasons Discovery Communications dropped a cool $12 billion to acquire it, along with its cable siblings the Food

Network and Travel Channel, in early 2018. One of the most popular shows on its lineup—*Flip or Flop* (starring the aforementioned Ms. El Moussa and her ex-husband Tarek) spawned spin-offs in Vegas, Nashville, Chicago, and Atlanta, and, as you might expect, wannabe flippers nationwide.

In fact, flipped houses—defined as property sold twice within a twelve-month period—aren't new. Flipping was hugely popular before the housing bubble popped, tailed off after, but has come back strong with the number of homes flipped hitting new highs in 2016 and 2017. The fact that there aren't as many distressed properties waiting to be gussied up and resold has put the squeeze on profits of late, according to ATTOM Data Solutions, which tracks the industry. Meaning that, yes, this is yet another thing that isn't quite as easy as it looks on TV.

Which doesn't mean there isn't money to be made. Homes flipped in the third quarter of 2017 yielded an average gross profit of $66,448. Keep in mind, gross is profit before the quartz (or laminate) counters go in; it's before you find the asbestos in the basement. Mindy Jensen, community manager of BiggerPockets.com, an educational site for real estate investors, has been buying, renovating, and selling for two decades. She and her husband buy properties to fix up themselves, live in the houses while they're doing the work, and sell only after two years so that they don't have to pay any capital gains taxes. "It's great at the closing table," she says. "But living through it is a hassle."

And that's not the only challenge. "Finding a house to flip is difficult right now because everybody wants to flip a house," she explains. "Finding a contractor who can do good work, on time and on budget [is impossible]. Pick two, you can't have all three." Jensen learned to do a lot of the work herself because finding contractors was so hard.

Recognizing how much work and money to put into a project comes with its own learning curve. "A house that has a lot of dark paint and ugly carpeting and old cabinets in the kitchen is not a difficult rehab," she says. Moving walls can be a different story. At the same time, you have to be careful you're not over-improving a property in a neighborhood that won't allow you to recoup your investment. "If everybody you're competing with has laminate countertops, maybe granite is not where you want to put your money."

Finally, HGTV hosts notwithstanding, you should know going in that the flipping world is not exactly estrogen saturated. The BiggerPockets audience—which is fairly typical of this field—is approximately 70 percent male, 30 percent female. "All the contractors are men. Some of them are much older. There's a lot of looking down on you because you're a woman or assuming you don't understand [what you're asking for]," says Jensen. "With a stock, you just buy a stock. With investing in real estate—especially the more hands on you are—you find some real Neanderthals."

BUYING INVESTMENT PROPERTY . . . TO KEEP

If buying and flipping houses falls into the category of Get Rich Quick real estate, buying houses or apartments you plan to rent are Get Rich Slow. Done correctly, however, owning rental real estate can provide a steady stream of income that can carry you through—and well beyond—your working years.

Sharon Vornholt, a real estate investor who writes and runs the *Louisville Gals Real Estate Blog* isn't encouraging anyone to give up their retirement funds. But she does try to cultivate another line of thought. "How many paid-off houses do you need to generate the passive income you need to live the life you want?" she asks. In other words, how much income do you want or need a month to sustain your lifestyle? "In Kentucky, if you have an average rental—a three-bedroom, two-bath ranch—you could hope to net $1,000 a month. If you have ten of those when you retire, you'll have $120,000 a year to add to whatever you save for retirement."

She makes it sound too easy, of course. There's work involved in learning about the financing, the legality of rental agreements, the ins and outs of property maintenance and management (whether you do it yourself or hire someone to do it for you). There's risk, too, and not just the toilet-backing-up-in-the-middle-of-the-night variety, but vacancies that are hard to fill, and tenants who don't pay and prove tough to evict. Overall, though, SparkRental's Denise Supplee, an owner of rentals herself, encourages other women to explore it. "If you get the right tenant in your property, they're paying the mortgage, they're paying the taxes and your expenses, basically, so you're building up equity in a property without even paying for it. [Yes,] there are issues that come along with it, but there are things you can do to minimize those issues. I'd say it's a win-win." If you're thinking of going down this road, here are a few suggestions.

THE RULES OF RENTAL PROPERTIES

- **Decide what you're looking for.** Many people buy rental real estate for cash flow or an income stream. Others are looking for appreciation. Let that drive your choice of market. If you're looking for appreciation, hedging your bets means being in a market—or at least neighborhood—that is growing, preferably at a nice clip. Cash flow is easier to come by. You can buy a house or apartment for $80,000, collect $800 a month in rent. If you sell it in ten years for the same $80,000, you've still taken in $96,000 and paid off a good chunk of your mortgage.

- **Get an education.** Investment real estate comes with a language all its own. You'll need to understand everything from property taxes to vacancy rates to capital expenditures (large, infrequent repairs like a new roof) and how to account for them. Screening tenants—which involves checking credit and employment history—can be challenging, but prevents a lot of headaches down the road. If you're not going to do all of these things yourself, you'll have to find and pay a reputable property manager to do it for you. (Some of these come packaged with turnkey companies that not only manage properties but also find the investments for you. Be careful of the high fees associated with these. Overpaying is a problem.)

- **Start with one property within an hour of where you live.** You tend to be more knowledgeable about the area around home. That helps with everything from assessing deals to hiring a plumber or electrician. Research properties online, then start driving neighborhood by neighborhood to get a feel for the place. It's also easier to keep eyes on your investment, making sure the lawn has been mowed or the leaves raked. Don't be overwhelmed by bargains, cautions Denise Supplee. "First-time investors tend to go for the cheapest properties. Often they end up being in not-so-great neighborhoods, and that's not a good place for beginners."

- **Aim to follow the 1 percent rule (or hew to local standards).** This says, essentially, you should aim to rent your new property for 1 percent (per month) of whatever you pay for it. A $100,000 price tag = $1,000 in monthly rent. It's pretty easy to do this in the middle of the country, much harder in hot markets like Denver or on the coasts. But, as the hosts of the *BiggerPockets* podcast like to say, within an hour-and-a-half drive of wherever you are, you can probably get closer to the 1 percent rule.

- **Remember: You're not living there.** Buying a home or apartment to rent to someone else is not the same as buying a place you'd want to live in. Keep in mind who your likely renter is: A single or a couple with no kids? One or two bedrooms is fine. Once you're looking at families, the number of bedrooms climbs to a minimum of three.

· **Plow the profits back into your properties.** While you're in the process of paying off a mortgage, any additional money you make (after taxes) should go into a fund that you put right back into your houses. Even if you don't need the money for maintenance in year one, you will eventually.

· **Create a timeline in sync with your goal.** Say you're looking at these properties as a way to help fund your retirement. If you buy your first at age 40, aim to pay off the mortgage in twenty years. That will position you nicely as you want to start scaling back on your day job.

· **Find some good mentors.** There is a lot of good information—online and off—about investing in real estate, and many people willing to take you by the hand and help you. Real estate investment associations or clubs (which exist in many cities) can be an entrée to some of these folks as well as lawyers, accountants, and property managers. Note: Some of these clubs are set up to help and some are set up to sell you high-priced courses in how to buy/rent/flip real estate. Be *very* cautious.

~

FINANCING IT ALL

Shopping for a home—surfing the listings, visiting open houses, peeking in closets—is fun. Shopping for financing for that home? Not so much. But make no mistake, it's every bit as important. We've gone through four different types of real estate purchases in this chapter and they're each a little different in terms of how you approach the financing. Here's a guide.

- Primary residence. You can buy a first home with a down payment as small as 3.5 percent of the purchase price, though some traditional lenders still require 10 percent or 20 percent. The interest rates on mortgages for first homes are lower than the rest of the loans on this list because they're less risky. If you get into financial hot water, you'll try really hard to continue to pay because it keeps a roof over your head. When you're shopping for a loan—and you should *shop* banks, credit unions, and online lenders—you'll be asked to make a few decisions. Do you want a fixed-rate loan or a variable one (or an ARM, adjustable rate mortgage)? If this is a forever house, a fixed-rate loan is generally the way to go. If you think you'll be moving in five, seven, or ten years, take an ARM timed to that scenario where the rate is fixed for the first five, seven, or ten years and then begins adjusting. If you go with a fixed-rate loan, do you want a thirty-year loan or a fifteen-year loan? The latter will be about 20 percent more expensive, but will save you considerably in interest overall. If you can afford that, it may make sense—particularly if in about fifteen years you'll be looking at retirement.

- Second home. Down-payment requirements on second/vacation homes are higher, generally at least 10 percent and often 20 percent. About 20 percent of buyers borrow equity from their first homes to buy their second homes (something to think carefully about given everything we learned when the housing bubble popped). Interest rates are generally slightly higher on second homes than first, but not always and not across the board. It pays to do the same careful shopping around you'd do with a first mortgage. Unlike with a primary home loan, lenders may also want to see that you've got enough cash on hand to manage anywhere from a couple of months to a half year's worth of payments if you were to lose your job.

- Rental property. You'll have to put down at least 20 percent, sometimes more. Mortgage rates for investment properties are generally 1–3 percentage points higher than those for primary residences, and you may pay an additional 1 percent in fees called "points." As you accumulate more properties, the requirements get tighter. A program from Fannie Mae allows borrowers to have up to nine mortgages at once, but it asks for down payments of 25 percent to 30 percent, six months' worth of payments held in a cash reserve account, and a credit score of at least 720.

- Home to flip. Interest costs are significantly higher in the riskier home-flipping segment of the market, climbing into the low double digits, not including a couple of points. Banks aren't the primary source of financing for flippers, other flippers are. Get educated by the real estate investors in your area, watch the deal flow, and do the profit-and-loss math before you dive in.

What Have We Learned

- *Owning a home represents a big step toward security for women today, regardless of marital status. Paying that home off is a step in the right direction, as the equity you rack up represents an additional chunk of money for retirement.*

- *As you accumulate wealth, owning a second home, whether it's a place you want to vacation or one in which you want to retire, may become an item on your to-do list. If you're planning to rent that home out, pay attention to the tax rules.*

- *If you're considering investing in rental properties and buying homes to flip, take the time to get seriously educated about what you're in for. The first can help provide a nice source of income, the second nice chunks of profit that you can turn around and reinvest, but both can be full-time jobs.*

Where Do We Go from Here

How else do we use our money besides saving it, investing it, and using it to buy things like homes that appreciate over time? We spend it! Research shows we have decidedly mixed feelings about that. It's time to allow our inner consumer to find some bliss.

CHAPTER 9

The Joy of Spending

I spend money because . . . I can. And it feels f***ing
awesome. Seriously. It is amazing to know that I don't have
to look at my bank account. I can buy that $300 dress, no
problem. I've come a long way.

—Anna, 50s, lawyer, divorced

        ~

In my house we sometimes say, "This is why we work." We say it to justify paying way too much for *Hamilton* tickets. We say it when we take a car to the airport because it's a lot less hassle than driving. I say it (to myself) when I'm getting my hair blown out even though I don't have anywhere special to go.

And while I'm fessing up, I've got to tell you there's a paragraph in this book that's been giving me pause. You haven't read it yet. It's coming up in the chapter on raising kids who launch. And it talks about how shopping for sport is one of those things you shouldn't do if you don't want to raise kids who are materialistic. Confession time: I shop for sport. To me, it's fun. Looking at things, touching things, trying things on—even if I don't buy *anything*—is a pleasant way to spend an afternoon. There, I said it. (And I feel better now.)

And yet, spending money is a strangely contentious issue. According to *Money* magazine's 2014 "Love and Money" survey, frivolous spending was the biggest flashpoint when it came to inciting money spats—and partners blame each other for having the problematic spending habit rather than looking inward. Perhaps that's because when we do take a closer look at ourselves and our spending behavior, it brings on a case of the guilt. A survey of mothers from 2017 by Babycenter.com found 57 percent feel guilty about spending money on themselves.

The "weird" morality around spending is something entrepreneurship coach Karen Southall Watts discusses in the college humanities course she teaches. "Sometimes we look at people's purchases or what they're wearing and what they're choosing to do with their money and decide that it's appropriate for us to make a moral judgment about them," she says. "Women are highly attuned to this dynamic, and no one wants to be on the receiving end of those comments. That's why there's guilt around buying things for you. It's a self-protecting mechanism."

Guilt, as we've already discussed in this book, doesn't get us anywhere. And so, the purpose of this chapter is to open us all up to the fact that spending can be a joy. It can be a pleasure. And, when you look at all the time and effort we put into buying things anyway, isn't that a better way to view it? Women already do 85 percent of the spending in the US. Both the overall number and the percentage of large purchases we make are rising. And it's not just millennials doing the buying. A 2018 report from J. Walter Thompson Intelligence calls British women over 50 the new "power consumers" because they're outspending their younger counterparts.

Here are just some of the things that women buy, according to the Yankelovich *Monitor* and Greenfield Online.

- 91 percent of new homes
- 66 percent of computers
- 92 percent of vacations
- 80 percent of healthcare
- 65 percent of new cars
- 93 percent of food
- 3 percent of over-the-counter drugs

So how do we wrap our arms around our spending like—as Olaf says—a big warm hug? How do we let go[8] of both the judging and the remorse? It helps to understand *why* we're spending and then try to align the flow of those dollars with our values. We talked a bit about this in Chapter 1 when we asked the question: What do you want from your money? Sometimes we want security or one of the other S factors. Sometimes, as we'll discuss in the final chapter, we want to make the

☛ Yes, I just took my two nieces to see *Frozen* on Broadway—a purchase, by the way, I do not regret at all. I do, however, regret the fact that it's been over a week and the earworm that is "Let It Go" is still playing on repeat in my head. "A kingdom of isolation. And it looks like I'm the queen."

world a better place—for people we know, or people we don't. But sometimes what we want is joy. We want to live it up a bit, and we want to use our money to help us.

THE HAPPINESS FACTOR

There has been a lot written on the topic of money and happiness—including an entire book on the subject by me. Here's the literature in a nutshell: The old saw that money can't buy happiness isn't exactly true. If you're struggling economically—paying your bills isn't easy, debt has you down—more money can absolutely buy happiness. It reduces worry. It relieves stress. If you're already living comfortably, on the other hand—you've got a nice place to live, a reliable car that gets you where you need to go, the ability to eat out and take the occasional vacation, and you're able to save something—more money doesn't typically buy much of a happiness boost.

How much it takes to achieve that comfortable life varies, of course, based on where you live and the people you're surrounded by (as we discussed in the chapter on relationships, it's not happy-making to put yourself in a scenario where measuring up is a constant challenge). The research of Nobel Prize winner Daniel Kahneman put the number at around $75,000. Economist David Clingingsmith of Cleveland's Case Western Reserve University got a little more granular. His research says after you hit $80,000 the positive impact of more money starts to tail off until you hit $200,000—after which it disappears completely. "For the most part, you'd get a bit more happiness for every additional dollar, but the amount of additional happiness goes down as you get richer," he says.

It's also important to note that—again, once you've achieved those basic comforts—more money may provide a short-term happiness boost, but it doesn't generally provide a long-term one. You've seen this if you ever got a significant raise. It makes a difference for a while but eventually you get used to the new level of affluence. You spend to meet the additional dollars in your paycheck. Eventually, you can no longer remember how you ever lived on less and your happiness settles back where it was.

This is a phenomenon that behavioral psychologists call hedonic adaptation. Think of it as reversion to the mean, where the mean is your average level of happiness. Good things can happen. Bad things can happen. And, generally, you end up right back where you were. (This is true, research has found, even of people who suffer life-altering injuries such as losing limbs. Eventually they wind up just as happy as they were before.) All of which does not mean that you can't use your money—however much you have—to bring more joy into your life and the lives of people important to you. You just have to be careful about how and what you spend it on.

Spend on Experiences, Not Things...

Think about a particular item of clothing you bought at this time last year. Something you really wanted. Perhaps it was a great dress or a pair of jeans that hugged in all the right places. You were thrilled to add it to your wardrobe *then*. But how are you feeling about it *now*? If just the thought lights you up or makes you want to make plans so you can don that particular piece, consider yourself lucky. Many things lose their luster over time. And it's not just fashions that fade, but technology, toys, accessories, kitchen countertops.

Spending money on experiences, however, tends to have a longer-lasting and more substantial payoff. Why? Experiences actually get better with time. When you experience something, you make memories. That allows you to go back and revisit, which brings the original burst of happiness you felt in the moment back to the fore. You may even embellish a bit and make it better than it was IRL. You'll see the picture on your Facebook timeline, or repost it yourself—#TBT—and get the warm fuzzies all over again.

Experiences also often involve planning. When you start fleshing out the details of that upcoming trip to, say, Nashville, researching which place to go to for barbecue and which for hot chicken, figuring out who's playing in town the night you're there, you start to get excited. Putting the dates on the calendar gives you something to look forward to. As Carly Simon sang back in 1971 (and the Heinz ketchup folks memorialized a few years later), the anticipation that's keeping you *way-ay-ay-ay-ay-ating* becomes part of the experience and you enjoy that, too.

The fact that experiences tend to rope in other people also works in their favor. The social aspect of being with others is, for most, a happiness plus. For Eliana, 30s, a lawyer in New York, that's date night, when she hires a sitter and reconnects with her hubby over a nice meal. "That feels luxurious to me and brings me joy." Harvard Business School professor Michael Norton, coauthor of the book *Happy Money: The Science of Happier Spending*, confirms that spending to strengthen relationships is (within reason) almost always a good use of money. "Take a friend out for lunch," he suggests. "The upside of that is that she'll probably reciprocate so you get two lunches. Humans are very reciprocal."

Finally, unlike things, experiences sometimes involve physical activity. Spending money to exercise can pay off in several happiness-boosting ways. First, it slashes stress. Fidelity and the Stanford University Center for Longevity collaborated on research that found humans experience, on average, four stressful life events each year—they can be good (having babies) or bad (losing a job) but they are all stressful. The study also found that one remedy helps reduce the stress in all of them: exercise. Get up. Get out. Move and sweat. In the short term, exercise makes you feel better because you blow off some steam. In the long term, it makes you physically stronger and more able to handle whatever stresses life is throwing your way. Even if you're not under particular stress, spending money on getting healthier can make you happier. That's what Carmen, 30s, a communications specialist from New Jersey, has found. "I recently joined a CrossFit class," she explains. "It's pretty expensive—around $250 a month—but it gives me confidence and makes me feel healthier, so that in turn makes me happier. I've looked for ways to cut $250 out of other monthly expenses, which is something I wouldn't have done in the past."

. . . Or Spend Money on Things You Experience

The other way to spend money on experiences is to buy things that are, well, experiential. A few summers ago, I bit the bullet and bought a stand-up paddleboard. Actually, I bought two. I had gone paddling with my friend Michele a couple of times, renting a board or borrowing one of hers. I had taken a couple of lessons. And not only could I get to my feet with relative ease (unlike my failed attempts at surfing), I loved it. Being out on the bay, watching schools of little fish swimming under my board, snooping at the homes that backed onto the water to see how their patio furniture was organized—I knew I'd never get tired of that. The first board was so that I could paddle myself whenever I wanted. The second was so I could do it with my daughter or a friend.

Those boards are things. But they are the sort of things that foster experiences. Whether it's a set of golf clubs so that you can get out on the back nine with your friends or your spouse, or a piece of art that brings you happiness every time you look at it, there are some things that are more than things. Replacing your charcoal grill with a gas one (purists hate this idea, I know, but stick with me) might inspire you to enjoy your backyard more during the summer because you don't have to wait forty-five minutes for it to heat up so that you can cook outside. Then again, if you like to have a cocktail while the coals are getting ready, flipping the scenario and going old-school charcoal instead of gas might be the ticket. The point is—for the biggest happiness boost—to think about how you'll integrate these experiential things into your life before you spend.

The only hitch here is that when you buy a thing to experience it, you actually have to use it. If you've ever bought an exercise bike that has turned into a clothes hanger, or a Vitamix collecting dust on a shelf, you know what I'm talking about. It's important to be realistic about your ability to follow through on your intentions. And if you find that you overpromised yourself, don't just let it sit there making you feel guilty. That's what Craigslist is for.

Spending When You Aren't Doing It Because It Brings You Joy

This seems like an appropriate time to raise the fact that we spend a lot of money that *doesn't* bring on a rush of positive emotions. Some of this, of course, is money we have to spend (and by *have to* I mean we don't have much of a choice). Paying property taxes doesn't exactly light my fire. Neither does loading up on bags of kibble from Wag. But I love both my pup and living in my house, so I view these purchases as the price of admission. They're just part of day-to-day life. But there are times we spend to make ourselves feel better, to regroup from a disappointment, or to extinguish a bad mood. "When I was a kid, my mother would take us shopping if we were having a bad day," says Kristin, 30s, the social media manager from Vermont. Today, she does the same as a pick-me-up for herself.

That sort of retail therapy can provide a short-lived boost, and it's fine as long as we understand what we're doing—and we stay within our means. It's when we overdo it that regrets ensue.

When we buy something that doesn't line up with our vision of how we should be spending, we experience a phenomenon called cognitive dissonance. We all have ideas of what kind of person we are—maybe we take pride in the fact that we're "smart shoppers" or great "bargain hunters." My friend Paige always smiles when she describes herself as "Scrubby Dutch," a term I had to Google. It refers to women on the South Side of St. Louis who used to scrub their concrete steps every Friday. South Siders are down-to-earth, innately frugal people, which is both how Paige sees herself and how she is. Even those of us who enjoy spending may have particular items on which we allow ourselves to splurge—theater, travel, handbags—because we rein it in elsewhere. But if we go out and spend money in a way that doesn't line up with that image of ourselves, we disappoint ourselves. And that leads to regret.

Georgette, 40s, who owns a tour bus company in New York, was raised with the belief that money was there to be saved and *not* to be enjoyed. "My parents said, 'Your grandparents left you this. And we're leaving you this.'" The idea was that the money always had to be carried down. It was never to be used for fun. To this day, she says, she doesn't buy as much as she could—or should. Even justifiable business clothing brings on a hesitation she knows came from her parents.

That's a shame, but it's not uncommon. Research has found that bigger purchases bring on bigger regrets *and*, lamentably, that those regrets can come on even if our purchases are perfectly within our financial means. So how can you avoid the nagging feeling that you *shouldn't have*?

Journaling about your purchase satisfaction can help you get a finer sense of your own feelings. For a month or two, keep a log of everything you spend money on. Just jot down what you buy and how much it costs. Then, a week or so after you make each purchase, go back and make note of how you're feeling about it in hindsight. Are you glad you did it? Do you wish you'd spent less? Not bought it at all? Dr. Mike Roizen, my coauthor on *AgeProof: Living Longer Without Running Out of Money or*

Breaking a Hip, used this tactic shortly after we put that book to bed. He found himself regretting the significant sums he was spending several times a week when he and his wife Nancy ate out with friends. To him it felt wasteful. They decided not to slash their outings, but instead chose more moderate restaurants. The result? All the fun for half the money.

You may also want to try visualization. Psychologist April Benson suggests thinking about where you'll put a particular item when you get it home. Even better, consider where it will be two months from now. How much pleasure will you be getting from it then? Will it be out of season and out of the rotation until this time next year? Or is this going to be a part of your everyday existence, and will you get pleasure every time you interact with it?

The other thing to consider is the chase. Or, rather, the excitement of the chase. A few years ago—as a sort of quasi New Year's Resolution—I vowed to stop shopping on sale. I had noticed that a disproportionate amount of un- or underworn things in my closets and drawers were things I picked up on sale. I live right outside of New York City, and New York City is the mecca of the sample sale.[9] So I made a point of monitoring my sample sale pulse and I discovered it was racing. Literally. I would see things I didn't really want at 50 percent or 75 percent off and buy them simply because they were discounted.

My new rule was that if I wasn't willing to buy it at full price, I couldn't buy it at all. For me, it's been a good filter. I've since allowed myself some leeway. But still, I ask the question: Would I buy it if it weren't on sale? If the answer is no, it stays in the store.

☛ For those of you who have never been, I feel compelled to tell you that sample sales are not what they used to be. When I first moved to New York in the 1980s, sample sales actually had *samples*—goods that designers were trying out to see if they worked and that, if you were willing to overlook their minor imperfections, could be picked up for a fraction of the retail price. These days, they're more overstocks and the deals aren't as great. But I sometimes go nonetheless.

THE FINE DIVIDING LINE

Spending joy quickly disintegrates into spending pain when it becomes *overspending*, which can be an issue even for six- and seven-figure earners. Chronic overspending robs you of those oh-so-important Ss: safety, security, savings. Choosing the smaller house or the older car in order to keep some extra money in your savings account may make you happier in the long term than making the purchase. Research published in the journal *Emotion* has shown that having more money in the bank is a better predictor of life satisfaction than income, indebtedness, or investments.

Sharon, 40s, the CEO of a speech therapy company in Portland, Oregon, has chosen to live her life well below her means for this reason. "I always had an opportunity to buy a more expensive car or buy a bigger house or have more stuff, but I always asked what was important to me. I never wanted to live to my maximum because I wanted to have choices."

That's been my MO as well. And I think—in this era where parking a third car in the driveway isn't a matter of whether you can afford the car, but whether you can afford the monthly payments—we should apply a slightly different lens of affordability to the purchases we choose to make. That lens is opportunity cost. The question we need to start asking ourselves is not only whether we can swing the purchase in the context of today's budget but also what having spent the money (or, committed to spending it) means for the choices we have tomorrow. If we commit to another few thousand dollars a year, does that limit the opportunities we have for travel, or giving back, or making a job change? It can be hard to do, because we may not be able to envision those future opportunities. But it's absolutely worth asking the questions.

But what about spending that's neither really overspending nor chronic? Some women beat themselves up about spending on things they want but that are not quite necessities. Others are in relationships where that kind of spending brings on tension. Having money that is yours to do with as you wish—and making sure your spouse or partner has a similar stash—can alleviate the relationship tension, as we talked about in Chapter 4. But a similar strategy can also work when the one giving you a hard time over your leisure spending is *you*.

Julie, 30s, a reading specialist in Pennsylvania, has set up a separate account for her fun money. Keeping it segregated, she says, allows her to do the things she enjoys without worrying about how to fund them—or feeling lousy about spending the money on them in hindsight. "I love to travel and explore new places, but the costs can add up quickly," she says. "When I have a particular destination in mind, I will purposefully set aside money for things like airfare, hotels, and meals out several months to a year in advance. This way, when my credit card bill comes in and is particularly high, I can transfer money to pay it off without any stress."

Eddie, 60s, a business development contractor in New Jersey, uses a similar methodology. "I set goals," she explains, most recently a very expensive camera. "I'm a photography enthusiast. So, first I sold old camera gear that I wasn't using and I started a savings account, and every time I got a bonus, I would put it in there. If I got a refund, I'd put it in there. Before I knew it, I had enough to cover the cost of the new camera." (Doing it this way, she notes, even the saving itself, watching the money add up, was fun.)

If you can give yourself over to the process, you may even find a sense of joy in the fact that the one doing this for you *is* you. "My dad came from Portugal when he was 17 and had nothing. And my mom grew up in Queens," says Jessica, 30s, a beauty marketer from New York who is expecting her first child. "I want to teach my kid that if you want something nice in life, you need to work really hard. And if you do buy nice things, you should feel validated because you did it yourself."

Time on the Clock

Another proven way to spend money to bring you joy is to use it to buy you time. We talked about this a little in Chapter 1, but let's get really granular. You can, even if you're not all that successful, acquire more money. You cannot, even if you're hugely successful, acquire more time. There are 24 hours in the day, 365 days in the year, 83 years in the average woman's life span, and so on. But, as my ex-husband likes to say: Assets are fungible. What you can do is use money to get other people to take tasks you don't particularly find joyful off your plate so that you don't have to do them. In other words, you can hire out.

"Time is an ultimately limited resource, but money is not," says productivity expert Laura Vanderkam. "As long as you're on track for retirement, we need to give ourselves permission to spend money as a tool to buy time. That's the scarcest resource—particularly in your child-raising years."

Amen to that.

There are those times, as financial coach Cindy Troianello notes, that using your own two hands to do things for yourself and your family feels really good. "People go out to dinner all the time," she says. "Going out to dinner or picking up food on the way home has to be five times more expensive than cooking yourself." But some people—including me—like to cook. I'd rather spend time prepping on a Saturday to have friends over for dinner that night than go to a restaurant. And it makes me feel good to cook the traditional foods at the Jewish holidays (preferably with my mother or my daughter). I wouldn't dream of ordering up a kugel or *kneidlach* (look it up).

What wouldn't I do? Garden (which I know many people love). Or iron (which my mother has always found surprisingly restorative). The point is that when you're choosing to trade time for money, it's as personal as any other financial choice. You should be selective in the tasks you decide to offload—but you also shouldn't allow anyone else to make you guilty for doing it. That's the conclusion Gina, 30s, a Pennsylvania market researcher with two kids, has come to. "It's been a big shift for me," she says. "Today I'm fine with having a housekeeper if it's going to make my life less stressful. That goes hand in hand with balancing a family. In fact, we were just discussing whether it made sense to start paying someone to start picking up the kids because that's going to get harder, too."

Finally, there is one *specific* thing we know makes for a more satisfying trade-off than others: a shorter commute. The commute—whether you drive, take the bus, or ride the rails—is the low point of many people's days. Or, as you may be more accustomed to thinking about it, the is-this-traffic-ever-going-to-let-up-because-I'm-already-late-for-my-meeting-and-I-still-need-caffeine? commute. Commuting sucks. Take it from a woman who's done it for the past 24 years. If you're looking for ways to build more time into your day, consider giving up a little space for a little more time (because shorter commutes = higher real estate prices) and you'll probably be happier. Alternatively, a lower-paying job that's closer to home and/or more flexible might do the trick. Or, notes Vanderkam, ask to telecommute a day or two a week. The expense of outfitting a home office is worth it to show your manager you've created a professional workspace that will allow you to get the job done; it can also make your work experience more of a daily pleasure.

SPEND ON OTHERS

There is one other way that spending has been proven to bring us joy: when we do it for others. Recently, I took Sasha, a soon-to-be 13-year-old, to a local jewelry store to pick out a gift for her upcoming Bat Mitzvah. She's been in my life since she was born, and I happen to know she's picky about what she wears. I didn't want to buy her something that would just sit in a drawer. Watching her consider pairs of earrings and then try on some necklaces was really fun. And seeing her face light up when she put on the one with the sparkly peace sign that clearly had her name on it lit me up inside as well.

The technical term for this is *prosocial spending*. Harvard's Michael Norton and some of his colleagues ran an experiment where they gave participants a small sum of money (some people got $5, others got $20). They directed half the subjects to spend the money on themselves and half to spend the money on someone else. At the end of the day, the people who spent on others felt happier than those who bought or did something for themselves. And interestingly, though people thought they would be happier spending more money, the amount didn't matter at all. (Which means: it *is* the thought that counts!)

Other research has demonstrated a strong link between happiness and giving money to charity. But what Norton's experiment shows is that the efforts don't have to be strictly charitable for them to produce joy. Gifts have a similar impact. And we can see that impact in children as young as toddlers, whom researchers have observed in the act of giving away some of their treats to others. A couple of things to keep in mind: Whether you're giving to a charity or to a person in your life, the happiness boost is bigger when you feel as if you have a choice about whether to do it. That's why when you feel forced to contribute to the office gift for a person you don't really like, it doesn't bring on a rush of warm feelings. You also get more joy overall when the spending helps you build a stronger relationship with either the person or the cause you care about. In that way, it really is about you after all.

What Have We Learned

- *Women spend the lion's share of the money—and it's not just millennials swiping their plastic, but women over 50 as well.*

- *There are specific ways to spend that make you feel good about doing it, in particular buying experiences over things (or things that function as experiences) and spending money on others.*

- *Using money to buy you more time is also a valuable strategy, as long as you're taking things off your plate that you dislike. If you can reduce the time you spend commuting, that's a home run.*

Where Do We Go from Here

In Part III, we'll look at using the financial stability and success you've created to build the life you want for yourself and the people you love by raising kids who become financially independent, caring for parents if and when they need you to, and crafting a legacy for yourself. This is the payoff for all the hard work you've put in.

⤬

You Using Money: To Create the Life You Want

CHAPTER 10

Raising Kids Who Launch and Flourish

Here's a snippet from the HerMoney Happy Hour in Philadelphia:

LISA: *(50s, entrepreneur, recently divorced): What changed most significantly for me was getting myself out of paying for my young adult children. I no longer pay for their car insurance or their medical insurance. My son is about to go back on my cell phone plan because it'll save him money. We're on a family plan, but he's going to Venmo me money for the bills. Venmo is my favorite thing with my children. Really, it's my favorite thing. Because they have the money and pay me back right away.*

JEAN: *So, be specific here. How exactly did you do that?*

LISA: *We took a year's worth of money, for each of the kids, a year's worth of car insurance, cell phone bills, and medical bills and gave them lump sum checks and told them: Be smart. Two of them were, one of them wasn't.*

JEAN: *What happened to the one who wasn't?*

LISA: *He's living with me now.*

Ahhh, kids. I sound like my mother when I say that (and probably her mother, too). But there's no other relationship we have that's as layered as the one with our children. That's because, unlike the ones with our spouses, our parents, or our friends, we feel responsible—we *are* responsible—not just for the people they are today but for the ones they become tomorrow.

We also dream a little bigger for them than we do for ourselves. In Chapter 1, we asked: What do you want from your money? You'll remember that high on the list were the Ss: safety, security, savings, and so on. For our kids, we are already providing those Ss, which enables us to focus on loftier goals: health and happiness, of course, but also enough success and achievement that they can live as well if not better than they did when they were kids.

This notion that kids of every next generation will outearn their parents is a long-standing part of the American dream. We came to believe it *will* happen because it *has* happened for as long as we can remember. But many of us sense we're at the end of that time in history. "My life is so great compared with where I grew up. We didn't have the opportunity that the kids have here," says Amanda, 40s, a stay-at-home mother of three in San Francisco. "But I think my kids are going to be frustrated that they can't live as well as we live now."

Still, we hold out hope that maybe they'll be among those who do prosper. So we enroll them in Musical Munchkins at 6 months and try to teach them to swim at 2. We give them language immersion, ballet or hip-hop, and sports—one for each season of the year. We supplement with private lessons when the batting isn't coming along as quickly as it should, and travel teams when we find a sport that suits. And that's all before we get to the academics, the tutors, SAT prep, college counselors, and essay readers. It's exhausting, but we've come to believe it's what we have to do—if only because everyone else is.

And yet, there is one S that we don't want: *spoiled*. Its sibling—*entitled*—is no picnic, either. And the kissing cousin—*materialistic*—may be even worse.

Materialistic people, simply speaking, value things more than cultural, intellectual, or spiritual pursuits, explains Tim Kasser, author of *The High Price of Materialism* and a professor of psychology at Knox College. This causes a laundry list of problems. People who are more materialistic are less happy, less satisfied with their lives, more depressed, and more anxious. They turn more to alcohol, cigarettes, and drugs to "self-soothe" away their unhappiness. They tend to be more competitive than cooperative and care more about themselves than the environment. The latest batch of research on the subject even shows that they're less engaged in learning and perform less well in school.

Sounds exactly like the sort of children you *don't* want to raise. And yet, depending on how you were raised, it can be hard to sidestep.

Jan, 40s, a mother of one from New York, says her earliest memories of money are all "nots." "Not having a lot of it. Not being able to go out to dinner. Not being able to go to the gift shop on vacation to get the teddy bear I wanted." As a result, she says, "I'm projecting to make sure my son has all of that." Sharon, the Portland CEO whose daughter is now 18, feels likewise: "Every prom, I was thrilled to buy her a new dress. [Still,] I wonder if I've taught my daughter the right lessons about money. She's not frivolous, but she's never had to figure out the real world."

Financial educator Susan Beacham hears these concerns from parents on a regular basis. They say, "I didn't have what my children have. I want to help them. How do I do it without ruining them?"

Ruining them. That's harsh. But it's also what makes the challenge so difficult. We want to give our kids the advantages that come with a comfortable life. Yet we don't want them to lose respect for those advantages or to not understand that they require hard work. And at the same time, we want to impart resilience so that when life does get hard, they will be able to cope, regroup, and move forward.

This is a hard line to walk. It requires us, as parents, to set financial limits that align with our values and to impose them without being disingenuous. Notes psychotherapist Eileen Gallo, coauthor of the book *Silver Spoon Kids*: "To say you can't afford it when you can afford it and your kids know that you can afford it doesn't play."

YOU ARE THE BEST (SOMETIMES ONLY) TEACHER THEY HAVE

Doing all of this is part of modern parenting. You can't count on school or Scouts or society to pass along even basic financial knowledge to your kids. Only seventeen states require a course in personal finance for high school graduation. (Don't get me started on how ridiculous this is.) And even if you live in one of those, it's still on you, because while a teacher can explain a budget or a credit score, a teacher can't pass along your values. Only you can do that.

And many of us aren't. According to the T. Rowe Price "Parents, Kids, and Money Survey," two-thirds of parents are reluctant to talk about money with their kids—many talk about it only when their kids ask about it. I'm not suggesting sitting your kids down at the kitchen table and having a capital *T* Talk but rather establishing a running dialogue throughout their lives. At 2, when they're in the grocery cart, you can explain why the choice of green beans over broccoli: because green beans are on sale. My Brooklynite sister-in-law Ali used weekend stoop sales to teach her twins that they could not just buy the toys they wanted on the cheap but also make money by selling the ones they were tired of. (Then one of those stoop-sale purchases brought bedbugs into the house and that was the end of that.)

Your children's asks for bigger purchases trigger a host of conversations: how to save for a longer-term goal, deciding what you really want and what you don't, working so that you can make more money faster, putting your money to work by investing it so that it can grow. Use your own history, tell them about your experiences—and be honest. When there's financial trouble in the air, kids tend to feel it. When parents talk in hushed tones about a colleague who lost a job and may have to move, they wonder: *Is that going to happen to me?* Psychiatrist Gail Saltz says that children are laser focused on one thing when it comes to money: *Am I going to be okay?* Assuming things are okay in your house, it's your job as a parent to convey that. And, if they're rocky—as they may be from time to time—to show your children that, although this year's summer vacation will be at a campground rather than a hotel, or even though you're downsizing because of a divorce, things will still be okay. *They* will still be okay.

There are two other overarching financial truths to keep in mind as you curate the conversations that shape their financial lives.

Truth 1: Money is relative.

How much we have isn't as important as whether we have more or less than the people around us. Just as you compare with colleagues, neighbors, and college classmates, your kids compare with friends, classmates, and teammates. And we all compare on social media. This will be true their entire lives, which makes getting comfortable with the fact that other people have more or less an important part of growing up.

Helping them reach this level of comfort is a far better strategy than doing whatever you can to enable them to compete. "Kids who get into trouble are kids who have nothing more to desire," says financial educator Jayne Pearl, author of *Kids, Wealth, and Consequences: Ensuring a Responsible Financial Future for the Next Generation*. "Everything is handed to them, they have no reason to have motivation or set goals. They can get into trouble because of that."

Truth 2: Money is finite.

No matter how much or how little we have, we have to choose how to allocate our resources—and our kids have to do the same. The closer we can line up those choices with our values, the happier we'll be. But our kids learn valuable lessons when we explain the whys behind our choices.

Which brings me back to the Volvo wagon I mentioned in an earlier chapter, a very nice car, by the way, but not a BMW. For years, I drove the latter, preferring the heavier steering to the loosey-goosey feel of some Japanese cars. Then I got separated, then divorced, and bought a Volvo. I didn't even realize it at the time, but like some of the women we heard from earlier, I saw a safe car as akin to the safety and security missing in other parts of my life. And nothing's safer than a Volvo. Unless it's a Volvo wagon.

My daughter, who was around 10 at the time, questioned the move. "You usually drive a nicer car," she said, or something to that effect. I explained that I was choosing safety over sizzle, citing the side airbags and the five-star safety ratings. I also told her I preferred the lower price tag, that I was choosing to put more into savings and spend less. If I'm remembering correctly, she rolled her eyes. (As I said, she was 10.)

I could have said, "It's my money." Although both valid and true, for the purpose of my child's financial education, that wouldn't have cut it. She still didn't like my car (much as she doesn't like its current incarnation). But she understood my rationale.

Girls vs. Boys

Importantly, we have to give the same detailed explanations to our daughters that we do to our sons. Lindsay, the jewelry company executive from outside San Francisco, recently experienced the death of her father-in-law, a wealthy man she describes as a waspy Don Corleone. "He took care of everyone—he had an ex-wife, a current wife, a son, a daughter," Lindsay says. "But he was also very traditional and sexist. So with his son, he said, 'I'm going to teach you everything you need to know to be a man of the world.' And with his wives and daughters, he said: 'You girls are going to be fine.'" When he died, Lindsay and her husband were left to pick up the pieces. "The sister was totally clueless. The wife was totally clueless. The ex-wife was totally clueless. Watching these three women be terrified—I felt so lucky because I have a clue."

Amazingly, as I write this in 2018, *this is still happening*. According to T. Rowe Price, 58 percent of boys say their parents are having conversations about financial goals with them, compared with 50 percent of girls; 12 percent of boys have credit cards, compared with 6 percent of girls; and more boys than girls are aware that their parents are saving for their college education.

Granted, we are not all zooming down that path. Emily, 50s, a single mom in New York who adopted her daughter at age 40, is doing her best to instill financial independence. "I tell her, 'Don't expect to marry someone. You need to be a woman who earns her own money.' I don't want her to have 20s and 30s where she pisses money away the way that I did."

But there is enough evidence—including a study of two thousand school-age children in England that shows boys age 5 to 16 receiving 20 percent to 30 percent more "pocket money" than girls—that it bears noting: Children tend to rise to the level of their parents' expectations. If we expect our daughters to be less capable with their money than our sons, they will be.

The Building Blocks of Financial Independence

Lesson 1: Teach them the difference between wants and needs.

As we discussed a few pages back, distinguishing between what's essential and what's extra can be tougher for our kids than it is for us. By providing for their basic (and not-so-basic) needs, everything on their list becomes a want. But you can get to the root of what's what by asking a single question: What happens if you don't have it? If it's a true need, the answers will reveal that.

Lesson 2: Teach them to choose.

Of course our children can have things they want. They just can't have them *all*. We set them up to succeed when they're little by giving them a couple of good options—the blue shirt or the green one, sneakers or sandals—and letting their choice stand. They learn that they have the power to make decisions that a) will be abided by and b) will be okay.

As they get older and the universe of choices gets larger, they need to understand that every choice comes with trade-offs. In middle school, for example, when language requirements kick in, they may be offered a choice of Spanish, French, maybe even Mandarin. If they come home excited about French—because that's what all their friends are taking—it's your job to sit down with them and explore the other options. After all, Spanish is spoken in more countries. Mandarin looks great on a college application.

What does making these sorts of choices have to do with money? Only everything. Fast-forward four years. Now your child is applying to college. Your offspring is brilliant, of course, so the acceptances are plentiful—but they're also wide-ranging. There's the honors program at the in-state school with reasonable tuition, the competitive private school that offered $21,000 a year in merit aid, and the elite private school that didn't. Making that choice means exploring trade-offs that will reverberate for years—which will be easier for your kids to do if they've been making decisions their whole lives.

Lesson 3: Teach them to tell themselves no.

The goal is to help them become self-regulating, to realize that they have the ability to say no to themselves. But this will never happen if you don't set and enforce limits to begin with. "When kids ask parents for things and parents say 'no,' they might feel guilty like they're depriving their kids," says Jayne Pearl. "Similarly, saying 'yes' feels like you're indulging them. But if you put your kids in charge of saying 'no,' it changes."

Every year psychotherapist Eileen Gallo takes her granddaughter shopping as a birthday treat. "I started when she got interested in clothes at age 11 or 12," she remembers. "I'd give her a budget and tell her we could spend $100 or $125." On one of their first outings, Gallo's granddaughter had her eye on white jeans. Their first stop was Bloomingdale's, where the white jeans she liked were $80—almost the whole budget. So instead of buying them, Gallo nudged her to keep looking. Eventually they found white jeans for less, got a few items to go with them, and her granddaughter learned a valuable lesson in shopping around.

This year her granddaughter turned 18 and started college. "I told her she had a budget of $250 and if she didn't spend it, she could have the cash," Gallo says. Instead of guiding her granddaughter, this year Gallo just watched as the young woman made measured, considered decisions on her own. "It was so affirming to be present with her while she was thinking through this. It was a wonderful experience," she says.

Lesson 4: Teach them to work toward a goal.

Just like adults, kids have things they want today, next week, next year. They need to learn to work their way there. If they set a pace that's too hard to keep, they'll fail, so encourage them not to take on too much too soon. And if they reach outside their financial grasp, consider lending a hand. If the gaming system they want, for example, costs so many weeks' allowance that you think they'll quit before they get there, offer to match the dollars they save so they can get there in half the time. In general, keep in mind that goals are most likely to be met if they're three things: specific, measurable, and attainable, which means broken into small enough chunks that they can actually hit, rather than big ones they can't. (And for those of you who are looking for info on the right way to do an allowance, I've got you covered. You'll find instructions on page 191.)

My son had his Bar Mitzvah right around Memorial Day and was due to leave for summer camp just over three weeks later. That gave him about twenty-one days to take his end-of-year exams, see all the home friends he'd be missing over the next eight weeks, eat all the home foods he might be missing even more, and—oh, yes—write about one hundred thank-you notes. The latter would have been a daunting number for most adults.

So, we approached it like any other goal. We got specific: all one hundred had to be done before he got on the camp bus. We made it measurable: we bought a roll of one hundred stamps so that he could measure and track his progress as the white strip they were stuck to got longer. And, by doing some quick division, we made it attainable: he'd write five a night before turning on the television or hitting the video games.

He not only did it, he wrote (and mailed) an extra one—to me.

Lesson 5: Teach them how to wait.

Working toward a goal goes hand in hand with an equally important financial lesson: the ability to wait. I can hear some of you thinking: *But my kid would have failed the Marshmallow Test.* For the uninitiated, the Marshmallow Test was a series of experiments conducted by psychologist Walter Mischel at Stanford University in the late 1960s and early 1970s. Children were offered the choice of one marshmallow immediately, or two marshmallows if they could wait for about fifteen minutes. The children who were able to wait later did better in school and on their SATs and had lower BMIs, all of which set them up for more success in later life.

What Mischel's research showed is that some children—some people—clearly tolerate delayed gratification better than others. But, as he explained to writer Jacoba Urist (whose 5-year-old flunked the test the night before she sat down with the psychologist) in a 2014 interview for the *Atlantic*, others can *learn* to wait. "So for adults and kids, self-control or the ability to delay gratification is like a muscle? You can choose to flex it or not?" she asked him. "Yes, absolutely," Mischel responded. "That's a perfectly reasonable analogy."

One of the best ways to get your kids flexing away is by encouraging them to get a part-time job. I'm a big believer in teens working. I buy into the research that shows kids can work up to fifteen hours a week without it interfering with their schoolwork. (Besides, no one is signing a contract. If you see their grades fall off a cliff, they quit.) My own study of five thousand Americans showed that adults who worked as kids are better managers of their own money.

Plus, my focus group of two (that would be my children) showed me that it often takes earning money to learn the real value of money. An allowance is well and good, but a dollar they earn is far more valuable than a dollar you give them. As my kids started bringing home their own bacon, I saw the synapses connect. A $70 football jersey was high on the list of my son's "wants" when I was paying for it. It fell to the middle when it was an allowance purchase for which he had to save. But when he equated it with two weekends' worth of babysitting and calculated that it cost *seven hours* of his time? All of a sudden the ones in his closet were just fine. And then there was this text exchange that followed the first pay period when he entered the workforce for real.

Him: Hey Mom. You know what's great?

Me: What?

Him: Getting paid!

Me: Congrats! You must feel great!

Him: You know what sucks?

Me: What?

Him: Taxes!

Add all of this encouragement up and what you get is the satisfaction you see in them when they reach for—and achieve—a big goal. When Jayne Pearl's son (now grown and making his living as a musician) was 6, he wanted a guitar and she bought him one. A few years later he wanted a specific acoustic guitar and she told him she'd pay for half. Eventually, he wanted an electric guitar, and Pearl told him he was on his own. "He saved up," she recalls. "And started crying hysterically when he was finally able to buy it. He was overwhelmed by the power of his own accomplishment." That's how you instill self-confidence and self-esteem, she notes.

Lesson 6: Teach them it's not the end of the world if they fail.

If you have children, you've had the coat fight. The temperature is headed down, so you tell your child as they're heading out the door: *Take a coat.* They rebuff you—*I'm fine, Mom*—you tussle, and eventually they head out, not wearing the coat, of course, but with it tucked under their arm. What happens if, when they rebuff you, you cave? Your child goes out. They're uncomfortable for a few hours. (They don't get sick. The *New England Journal of Medicine* has published research on that.) And perhaps they don't argue the next time. Because they learned.

This is how it should go with money. Our kids need to be allowed to make their own decisions and their own mistakes, and we need to not bail them out when they fail. According to the aforementioned T. Rowe Price study, when parents let kids decide when to save and spend their money on their own, those kids are less likely to spend money as soon as they get it, to lie to their parents about what they spend money on, and to expect parents to buy them what they want.

Living with their choices, and the mistakes that sometimes result from them, should start early. When they choose popcorn at the movie, there's no deciding they want candy halfway through. As they age, the choices—which video game, which phone, which college—grow in size, scope, and price tag. And they need to understand that, although there are some things you can return to the store for a full refund, with others there's no going back. If you constantly save them from the pain of having chosen badly with the smaller, less significant items, they'll be at a loss for how to handle it when they screw up with the big ones.

AN ALLOWANCE THAT WORKS

In order to learn to manage money, kids need to have money to manage. Giving a regular allowance is one way to put money in their hands. The problem with an allowance is that many parents don't use it effectively.

Think about the lessons we're trying to impart in this chapter: Money is finite. You have to make choices. There may be no do-overs. If you give an allowance and then continue to pay for everything your kids want, you've botched the opportunity. Instead, you need to require your kids to start to pay for things they want, and you need to *not* give them enough to buy them all so that they have to choose.

So, rather than starting with a number, start with a list. What are you going to expect your kids to buy with their money? For the young ones, candy at the grocery store checkout? Today's equivalent of Pokémon cards (I actually think some kids still want Pokémon cards)? As they get older, manicures? Gifts for their friends? Video games? Older still, gas in the car? Meals out with their friends? Lunch during the day if they'd rather not pack it? Clothes?

Once you've figured out what the list encompasses, figure out how many of those items you're willing to buy per week and price them out. That's your base allowance number. If the allowance is supposed to cover lunch at school—and lunch is not something you want them to skip—then add on an amount for discretionary spending. If all the items on your list are wants, not needs, you don't have to pad as much.

As your children age, the items on the list should grow and so should the amount you give in allowance. The goal is that when they head off to college, they're equipped to handle a month's or a semester's worth of spending money at a time—and not blow it all in the first couple of weeks.

Finally, a word about payday. I was a lousy allowance giver. I never seemed to have the cash, and so when my kids would come after me with an accusation that I owed them for several weeks, I always figured they were right and paid up. I'm sure it cost me. It also wasn't particularly effective. So, when my daughter was 12 and my son 15, I started giving them their allowance electronically. I opened savings accounts, linked to mine, at our bank and set up automatic weekly transfers from my account to theirs. Before they were able to drive to the bank, I functioned as the ATM. If they needed cash, we'd sit down, sign in to our accounts together, transfer money back from them to me, and I'd give them the bills. The bonus was that long before they headed to college, they were comfortable not just pulling money from the ATM but putting birthday checks—and eventually part-time and summer job paychecks—into it as well. And as they moved into lives and jobs of their own, they continued to use this system we established, and, at least for a little while, I was able to monitor from afar.

You Can't Teach What You Don't Do

My friend Becky—like me and many of the other women I know—rises with a cup of coffee (or two) and unwinds with a glass of wine at night. One day, her teenage son, emboldened by what he learned in his health class, said, "You know, Mom. You start every day with a stimulant and end it every day with a depressant." Becky knew this already. And, by the way, she (and I) are just fine with that.

The point is that kids don't miss a thing. They don't just learn about money from the financial lessons we tell them, they learn about money by watching our every move. Remember the money stories from Part I? You create your child's every day. When we model good savings behavior, our kids are more likely to be good savers as well. If we're preaching saving but simultaneously spend our weekends shopping for sport? Not so much.

Research has found that just like secondhand smoke is bad for our kids, secondhand materialism may be, too. The more we model the values we want to see in our kids—making time for people we care about (including them) and causes we believe in—the greater the antidote we've given them to resist their materialistic impulses.

Finally, while you're modeling that better behavior, take a stab at modeling how you handle it when you make financial mistakes. We all make them. So pull off the Band-Aid and share the regret, the lessons, even the embarrassment with your kids. My kids are way too familiar with my stories about pulling money out of an early 401(k) and buying an answering machine from a guy on the street in 1987. At $20, I thought it was a steal. It turned out to be a brick. (They think the fact that I carried the brick around all day before opening the box is hilarious.) *What* you're sharing is not as crucial as *that* you're sharing. When they can see that you've made financial mistakes and you're okay, it allows them to believe they can make them and be okay as well.

LET THEM EXPERIENCE GIVING BACK

Years ago—so many years that I don't remember the context of the conversation—Anne, a woman in my community who was part of the constellation George H. W. Bush called the thousand points of light (his description of America's volunteer and charitable organizations spread "like stars...in a broad and peaceful sky"), explained to me why she was so involved in and devoted to the charities she had chosen to support. And she did it in one sentence. "I was raised this way."

There's something to that. If you want your kids to be givers, you need to raise them to be givers. The more affluent their surroundings, the more important this becomes. Zoe, 40s, a mother of two and director of a nonprofit organization in New York, understands this: "We live in an affluent suburb [so I wanted my kids to] know that we have more than enough to give away." Her solution—which she began when her kids were 5—was to take half the presents her children received for their birthdays and stash them away. At Christmas, they'd deliver those new toys to the local Ronald McDonald House. She chose that charity because it allowed her kids to go where the presents were being donated and see it—as opposed to others where you just dropped them in a box.

That Zoe did this in a way her children could understand is a big deal. Financial educator Susan Beacham has seen similarly good intentions sometimes run amok. In her community, some parents request charitable donations instead of gifts for their young children's birthday parties. "I'll be giving workshops and parents will say, 'Johnny, tell Mrs. Beacham about how we donated money.' The kids look at the parents confused and the parent prompts with the name of the charity, then the kid parrots it back to me." It's clear that the child often has no idea what the charity does and has probably never been there. "Parents trip over their own wonderful intentions when they forget to include the child in the charity. It's experience where they can watch you—not just listen to your words—that's going to teach them," she says.

Go for Launch

Add it all up and what you hope to achieve is a smooth launch into adulthood—which doesn't mean a launch without a hitch but, overall, an experience in which your children eventually do get to financial independence.

To do that, we have to let go. That can be hard. As I was writing this chapter, my son's car was stolen out of the garage below his apartment building. Of course, he had auto insurance as well as renter's insurance to cover the belongings he'd stashed in the backseat. But he was understandably upset. He felt violated. I knew that feeling—in my early 20s, a suitcase containing a good chunk of my possessions was swiped out of the trunk of a friend's car. And he had it worse; they had taken the whole vehicle. I felt helpless, so I tried to help by throwing money at the problem. "Go on Amazon," I told him. "I'll get you a backpack and headphones to replace the ones that were taken." "No, Mom," he said. "I don't think I should have such nice things if they're just going to get stolen. Besides, if I want them, I can buy them. I make money now."

That's what it sounds like when independence is asserted. I backed off. Point taken. Because that's what we—as parents—should want.

Still, launching is a bit of a dance. Even once the nest is empty, you still might be financially supporting your children, in ways both big (24 percent of us help with rent, according to 2017 research from CreditCards.com) and small (39 percent of us still pay the cell phone bill).

Are there downsides of maintaining this sort of financial support? What is the right time to cut those last financial ties, and what financial benchmarks should your kids hit first? Moving our kids off the dole requires two sets of information, says Ruth Nemzoff, author of *Don't Bite Your Tongue: How to Foster Rewarding Relationships with Your Adult Children*. First, you need to know tactically what you're paying for (many parents don't), and second, you need to know what you're trying to accomplish with that money. Is it a gift? A bribe? An incentive? Or an enabler? Once you understand your own motivations, it's easier to make changes. Here are five important steps to take.

Step 1: Survey the situation.

Look at your own financial needs, emotional needs, and expectations. Look at your child's financial needs, emotional needs, and expectations. And look at the landscape. An adult child who has returned home temporarily after a divorce or a layoff is a different story than a college grad who has been living under your roof for two years because they haven't found the perfect job. In the latter scenario, you have to ask whether you're enabling your child to be overly picky when they should take the next paycheck that comes along.

Step 2: Be transparent.

Whatever you decide you're willing to pay for—and you're not willing to pay for—be up front with your children about it. Lisa, 50s, who runs a health and wellness business in Wisconsin, was ultra-specific with her college-age son. "We made an agreement that his job was to be a student and take his university years seriously," she explains. "We would pay his tuition if he got a good grade point average. We want him to learn a work ethic, so he's been responsible for [his spending money]. And with things like his car insurance, we pay. But he knows if he gets a ticket, he's going to pay the incremental difference in premiums."

Step 3: Let them know change is coming.

Whether you're about to cut back on the monthly stipend you're giving your child or are ready for them to move out, give a good six months' notice that it's coming. That gives them enough time to understand that they're going to need to either increase their overall earning or decrease their overall spending in order to absorb these costs. Tell them why this is happening—you don't have to defend your reasons; after all, it's your money—but the why is important. If you feel like you're hurting their chances of living independently by continuing to offer support, say so. If you can no longer afford to do it because you need to put the money into caring for Grandma or your own retirement stash, say that.

Step 4: Help them build a budget.

Or, at least offer to. I did this with my son's former girlfriend when she graduated from college, and then again with him. You can use an app, like Mint, or just pencil and paper to help them figure out where their money is going today by sitting down with their monthly paychecks and bills, and following the cash flows. In doing this, be open to the fact that their lives may not work like yours. My son—who has a car—budgeted $250 a month for Uber. Why? Because when he goes out with his friends on the weekends, they drink. So, they don't drive. I was perfectly fine with that. And let them know, if they run into stumbling blocks, that you're always there to revisit it again.

Step 5: Embrace technology.

Finally, there will be cases where it makes sense, for instance, for your kids to remain on the family cell phone plan in order to save the overall family money. Venmo and Zelle, which allow you to bill each other rather than asking for the money month after month, are godsends. Your kids are likely already using these platforms with their friends, so they're used to being electronically nudged and won't take offense.

What Have We Learned

- *It's part of a parent's job to give children a financial education—whether we want to or not—and the best way to begin is by making money part of the daily conversation at home.*

- *The most important lesson children of all ages need to understand is that money is finite, and they need to choose how to allocate their resources.*

- *As you get ready to launch your kids toward independence, you need to prepare your kids for what's to come so that they can accept and get ready for this new phase in their lives.*

Where Do We Go from Here

One big benefit of longer lives is that many of us get to enjoy more years with our parents and other older relatives. But as they age, they may also need help tactically and financially to manage. And they (and others) will likely look to you, as their daughter, to provide it.

CHAPTER 11

Caring for Your Older Parents

In the middle of December 2017, I noticed my mother sniffling during our daily phone calls. A week later she had a hacking cough. And by the time Christmas came and went, it was the full-blown flu and my stepfather, Bob, had it, too.

Now, the flu is worrisome enough in older people, but this was the flu season to end all flu seasons. Doctors were hospitalizing patients with regularity. There was a run on Tamiflu. But my mom and Bob have good doctors in Florida, where they live during the colder months. They also have a robust community of friends and family—it seems like most of their Philadelphia neighborhood makes the pilgrimage and that I'd get a call if I needed to be more concerned.

Then a close friend of theirs died suddenly and unexpectedly. Their whole Florida gang packed up to attend the Philadelphia funeral—except for my mom and Bob. The doctor said they were too sick to travel and though Bob was rallying, my mom sounded worse. I had already started mulling the options—get on a plane, bring in a nurse, talk to the doctor about having her admitted—when my phone started to ring.

Did I mention I have brothers?

There are the two younger ones—who, despite being fully grown, highly capable men and fathers, I will always refer to as my "middle" brother and my "little" brother. Since my father passed away and my mom married Bob, I also have three fully grown, very capable stepbrothers, one of whom is a doctor in LA. (If you are ever lucky enough to acquire stepsiblings in later life, I highly recommend that one be a doctor.)

Anyway, the point is: they all called *me*. They may have defaulted to me because my mother (as opposed to their father) was the sicker one. But they could have also just gone along with my brothers, who have done it their whole lives—because I am the oldest and the only girl. In my family, it has always been understood that I am *the one*.

Which is not to say that anyone was shirking responsibility. Every single one of us was willing to get on a plane to Florida—and said so. In fact, one of Bob's sons had the first boots on the ground. But it was also clear that I was the coordinator of care. I found the nurse who would check in on them twice a day through the long New Year's Eve weekend. I figured out grocery delivery via Instacart.

This was the first time I felt like a caregiver for my parents. Although my father was sick for five years before he died, my mother was fully in charge. And even though I am one of those women who is a natural problem solver, it was daunting. It was daunting to wonder if I was doing enough—or too much. Daunting to try to manage from 1,300 miles away. Daunting to spend the hours on the phone with those five men who were, quite clearly, just as scared as I was.

There is more of this to come—for me and for most of you. As our parents get older—even if what you're dealing with is a case of the flu that vanishes by February (whew!)—we need to understand that this is what lies ahead. And the sooner we can embrace it, and start planning for it, the better. Because we are all daughters, and daughters are *the ones*.

The Profile of a Caregiver

Caregivers are a huge and growing lot. More than 34 million Americans provide unpaid care for a family member or friend over age 50, according to AARP and the National Alliance for Caregiving. The average caregiver is a 49- or 50-year-old woman, typically working, with children of her own, who also spends twenty to twenty-five hours a week caring for other (female) relatives. Some are older. But many are also younger; nearly 10 million millennials are caregivers for parents and grandparents.

What do caregivers do? Only everything. Caregiving can involve a huge range of health-related tasks, and helping with what the insurance industry calls "activities of daily living"—bathing, feeding, dressing, grooming, toileting (yes, that's a word). But most caregivers also do day-to-day errands, housework, and home repairs and take on financial tasks like paying bills.

And the cost of this care is staggering. The estimated dollar value of the informal care that family and friends provide is $522 billion a year—more than total Medicaid spending. The average cost to each individual female family caregiver? Nearly $325,000 in lost wages, pensions, and Social Security, according to MetLife—not counting the $7,000 that seven out of ten caregivers spend annually *out of their own pockets* to cover other costs.

But those are just the statistics.

What gerontologist Mary Jo Saavedra sees in her practice is more of a dance. When women like us become the caregivers, the overarching characteristic is a determination to do the right thing. Every day she meets with women who are smart, savvy, educated, and ready to go into full swing to protect their parents and take care of them when they need it. That can be tough on the often equally competent, problem-solving mothers and fathers who raised us. "There's a natural tension that exists between children and their parents," says Saavedra, author of *Eldercare 101*. An adult who has always been the parent has no intention of giving up their decision-making power. It can be a threat to them, and they're going to fight it. "Meeting in the middle is where we want to find the magic," she says.

The only way to do that is to plan for it. Accept a) the fact that longer life spans mean caregiving is something you'll *likely* deal with at some point and b) the possibility that the costs may be large. "Really plan and budget for this, because it can be as big or as large as mortgage and rent now," Care.com CEO Sheila Marcelo said on the *HerMoney* podcast. "If you're not planning ahead, then it can really impact your career." And your life.

START THE CONVERSATION

"My mom is my best friend, so I talk to her about money," says Tracey, 30s, an attorney with two kids from New York. "I know that they've invested in long-term care insurance. I have a pretty good idea of their financial situation. And I think my brother knows a little bit more about their end-of-life plans."

Tracey is unusual. Not so much the best friend part. Since *Gilmore Girls* hit the small screen in 2000, we're hearing more Lorelai-and-Rory scenarios than ever. The talking about money part, though, is not happening nearly enough.

According to a 2016 study from Fidelity Investments (which surveyed both parents and their actual adult children), two-thirds of families disagree about when it's appropriate to tee up a discussion about parental finances, and more than one-third say it shouldn't be discussed until after retirement *and* until after health or finances become an issue. That is *way* too late, but Mary Jo Saavedra understands why it's happening. "It's never too early, but it always—100 percent of the time—feels like it's too early," she says. Perhaps that's why:

- While 69 percent of parents say they've had detailed discussions with their adult kids about wills and estate planning... 52 percent of children say they haven't.
- While 72 percent of parents expect that one of their adult children will step into the role of long-term caregiver if need be... 40 percent of the adult children identified as being that caregiver weren't aware of it.
- While 69 percent of parents expect that one of their adult kids will be the one to help manage their finances and investments... 36 percent of those adult children didn't know about it.

- And while 72 percent of adult children believe their parents should be tackling the issue of long-term care...just 41 percent actually are.

That disconnect is a big problem—for both generations. The problem with not having a full understanding of what's coming your way as far as your parents' needs are concerned is the toll it could take on *your own* financial security. Kathleen, 40s, a brand marketer in New York, is one of those in the dark. "I worry that my parents don't have their act together as much as they should," she says. "What would happen if they ended up depleting their savings and investments to pay for aging?" She has no idea what the answer to that question is, because they haven't discussed it.

But here's the thing. When we do start talking about it, almost *everyone*—93 percent of adult children and 95 percent of parents—feels significantly better.

So why are we so mute? Because it's *uncomfortable*. It's uncomfortable for parents because it requires facing their own mortality, acknowledging that perhaps they haven't been as financially savvy as they might have liked, and letting their children into very private areas of their lives. It's uncomfortable for adult children who don't want to be seen as moneygrubbing, don't want to insult their competent, independent parents, and don't want to face their parents' mortality, either.

You can understand why the messages that fly back and forth are as mixed as a batch of scrambled eggs. Research has shown that older parents want to maintain their autonomy and their independence—but also want their kids to be helpful and available. Parents are annoyed when their adult children try to help—but are also appreciative that they care enough to do it.

Put all of those reasons together, throw in some sibling rivalry, and you've got a massive roadblock on the way to having these conversations. The only way to smooth the path is to acknowledge the devastation that ensues if you *don't* have them. If we wait to begin talking about these things until the need is acute, we may be too emotional to make rational decisions—and not have the time to properly research and think through our options.

Emily, 50s, a business travel consultant in Eastchester, New York, saw how stressful that can be as she watched her parents care for her grandmother. "She went from her home to assisted living to living with my parents," she says. "Watching my parents decide when to dip into her disposable income had an impact on me. At what point do they hire someone to help? They waited until the last possible moment [to deal with all of it]. That was a huge lesson for me."

Okay—you get it. So how do you get this conversation going?

First, pick a time.

It should not be in the middle of an event that has any other tension brewing around it. Thanksgiving, while you're rushing around trying to make sure you have enough clean glasses to set the table? No. Two days before Thanksgiving, while you're leisurely scrubbing carrots to make ahead? Much, much better.

Second, find an entrée, a reason to start talking.

Elder law attorney Carolyn Rosenblatt suggests big birthdays like 65 or marker events like retirement. "They're very meaningful to the parents," she says. "They signal a change—and that's what the conversation needs to be about. The inevitable change of getting older."

As a journalist, I've long been a fan of the give-a-little-to-get-a-little form of interviewing. You start with: "Mom, I've just started to look at life insurance," or "Dad, I was going over my will." Essentially you're saying, *It's not about you, it's about me.* That should put them at ease immediately (they've been focused on you their whole lives). Reveal a few salient details, then say, "It made me realize we've never talked about your plans for the future," or something along those lines. It doesn't have to be perfect. It just has to be.

If you have nothing personal to fall back on, use the story of what happened to a friend or colleague—or bring up the news. Aretha

Franklin, Prince, Michael Jackson, and author Stieg Larsson famously died without wills. Robin Williams's family did battle over his estate. Mark and Priscilla Zuckerberg have pledged to donate 99 percent of their Facebook shares to charity. Three good conversation starters right there.

Third, cover the bases.

Among the questions to ask:

- What are your wishes for the future?
- Where do you want to live as you get older?
- Do you have a will/living trust/power of attorney/healthcare directives—and where would I find them?
- Who's on your financial/health team—and could you make a list of how I could contact them if I need to?
- Where are your important documents?
- Where are your accounts—and could you make a list for me (including passwords) of how I could get into them if I need to?
- How are you doing financially?
- Do you have long-term care insurance?

Those are, essentially, the nuts and bolts. But these discussions also need to explore the what-ifs:

- What if you were no longer able to take physical care of yourself? Where would you want to live then?
- What if there were no longer two of you? Have you thought about where you might be most comfortable?
- What if someone started to notice that you're slipping cognitively? Would you be willing to let us tell you about those concerns? And could we talk now about what you'd like to have happen next?

Fourth, keep the door open.

Ask: Can we talk about this again soon? In many respects, that last question is the most important one. You want to leave your parents with the impression that this is not one and done, rather this is something you'll need to keep talking about as things change through the years. They should know you're always ready for them to come to you, too.

What if you try—and get nowhere? Try invoking the 40/70 rule, which basically says that by the time adult kids are 40 or their parents are 70, they need to have at least started talking about these things. If that doesn't do the trick, enlist the help of a professional (their lawyer, accountant, or financial advisor, not yours). Set up a three-way meeting and, while letting the professional lead, put as many of your questions on the table as possible.

Siblings and the (Questionable) Family Meeting

A number of the professionals interviewed for this chapter invoked the importance of the family meeting, calling them a "critical piece" of the process. And yet, my mother hates them. Family meetings make her—and she believes many other people—feel ganged up on. It's clear that everyone else has been talking, planning, *scheming*, in advance. She would rather talk one-on-one with each of her children and then—if necessary—come together as a group.

Either way works, but if you are a sibling, there is absolutely no question that your brothers or sisters should be involved in any conversation about care or assistance. Getting everyone on the same page early minimizes conflict later and makes it easier to move quickly into action when necessary. It also avoids suspicion. Sibling rivalries die hard, if at all. Brothers and sisters may wonder if you (or whoever is in charge) are trying to gain a financial advantage. They may speak out to your parent about how they don't think your plans are the right plans, which can result in more stress on the one person you're trying hardest to help: the parent.

Besides, as almost all primary caregivers eventually discover, help is a good thing. And figuring out what role everyone is willing and able to play early on—and getting buy-in for the plan—is a crucial part of that. It may be very clear what those roles are. I have a financial reporter friend with one sister who is a doctor and one sister who is a lawyer. In their family, it's pretty easy to decide who handles the legal, the health, and the money. Usually the puzzle doesn't present itself so clearly, and you have to just decide.

But there does need to be one point person who can interface with the doctors and who is (preferably) close enough to go to appointments, ask questions, talk to hired caregivers who are in the picture. Generally, this should be the same person who has power of attorney over healthcare. If no one in your family can fill this role, you can hire a professional called a geriatric care manager (more on this in a bit).

The important message here is that—even though it's unpleasant— you have to do it. There may be disagreements and hurt feelings, but consider that dealing with them is like buying an insurance policy on the relationships with your siblings that will long outlive your parents. Or, as my dad used to invoke when the three of us were sniping at each other at the dinner table: *Rule #537: You better have each other's backs, because at the end of the day you only have each other.*

Use All Your Senses

The holidays—if they're happening at Mom's or Dad's (or Mom and Dad's)—are important for another reason, too. They give you a chance to see with your very own eyes how things are going. Which is why, if you haven't been there for a while, you should arrange to visit.

Parents never stop being parents. Just as you downplay the sinus infection with the 101-degree fever you've had for a week to your kids as "just a cold," many older parents don't want to trouble you with their ailments. (That's what lunch with their friends is for—or, as my stepfather calls it, "The Organ Recital.") They may also be worried that if they do let you have a peek, you'll start making moves to limit their independence.

Which is why you have to see—and smell, and touch (as in, how long has it been since this place has been dusted?)—for yourself. Don't feel bad about this. "You're not snooping," says Jane Wolf Frances, a social worker and psychotherapist who runs the website Parenting Our Parents. "You're acting like a responsible loving family [member] as you open the refrigerator. What's in there? What's missing? Look in the medicine chest. What are they taking? Who's prescribing it? How old is it?" Look at the house itself. Are there grab bars in the bathtubs? Do they seem to be living downstairs and not heading up as much as they used to?

Look specifically for piles of paper in the house. By age 70, 10 percent of people start to lose some of their cognitive functioning ability. By age 80, half have some sort of cognitive impairment. Finances are one of the first areas in which this trouble becomes apparent. So, look for bills piling up. Are they opened? Does it look as if they haven't been paid? Are there a lot of boxes, a signal that a lot of as-seen-on-TV or online shopping is happening? And are they hoarding cash? All are worrisome signs.

Finally, look at your parents themselves. How are they walking? Do they seem more frail than the last time you saw them? How is their mood? Their speech? Ask, point-blank, if they have fallen recently.

The last thing my stepbrother Gary (he would be the one with the dark sense of humor, also the doctor) says to our parents before he leaves is: Don't fall. Older Americans fall around thirty million times a year—yet often don't tell us about it because they think they're buying their own one-way ticket to the nursing home. It's true that falls are the number one cause of injuries in people over 65. It's also true that many are preventable. Gary has vanquished every throw rug. And we've all got portable grab bars in our showers for when Mom and Bob visit. (They attach with suction cups and are less than $15 on Amazon.)

The High Cost of Care

There's no getting around it: Care costs. According to Genworth, the median national annual cost for adult day care is $18,200, assisted living is $45,000, a home health aide is $49,192, and a private room in a nursing home is $97,455. Depending on where you live, it can sometimes cost significantly more. And while Age Wave research tells us that 63 percent of people over age 50 do not believe they'll need long-term care, 70 percent will.

So, while the starter question is "How are you doing financially?" or "How's the money holding out?" you really need to get at these nuts and bolts:

- How much money is there?
- How much income is there?
- How quickly are they spending—i.e., after they receive their Social Security and pension checks, how much are they pulling out of their nest egg to cover the gap?
- How much equity do they have in their home, and is there a remaining mortgage?
- Do they have other debts?
- Do they have long-term care insurance?

This conversation may feel invasive to you and them (I feel like I'm invading my mom's space just writing the questions—and she and I talk about it on a regular basis). Have it anyway. If you get one or two answers on the first go-round, take a break and try again in a week or so. Explain that you're doing this as much for you as you are for them—which, by the way, is true. You need to understand as early as possible what the shortfall is so that you can plan for it, with your siblings, and still take care of your own financial lives.

Once you've got a sense of whether there's a financial need, you can start planning for what you can contribute both physically and in dollars.

One mistake many family caregivers make is to measure the cost of care directly against their income. If the latter is equal or a little less, they quit to care for their parent. It's

often better for your long-term security to stay in the work-force, accruing retirement contributions and Social Security credits, and hire a professional caregiver—even if the current dollars are essentially a wash.

And pay attention to the cash flows as well. Age Wave notes that half of all caregivers don't track what they're spending. That's a mistake from both a planning (you can't control what you don't measure) and a tax perspective. If it gets to the point where you are providing more than 50 percent of financial support for your parent (even if your parent doesn't live with you), you may be able to claim them as a dependent on your taxes. You may also be eligible for the dependent care credit. And you may be able to write their medical expenses off as a deduction.

Should you purchase a long-term care policy for your parents as a way to hedge your bets? These policies are pricey. (The average cost for three years of care for a 60-year-old married couple is between $2,000 and $3,000 a year, and prices go up with age.) But if you, or you in combination with your siblings, can afford it, having a policy means not having to come up with the money to help later (or relying on benefits paid for by Medicaid, which are more limited than the services you have access to if you pay privately).

AND WHILE WE'RE TALKING ABOUT LONG-TERM CARE FOR YOUR PARENTS . . . HOW ABOUT FOR YOU?

A 65-year-old couple entering retirement can expect to spend an average of $280,000 just on unreimbursed healthcare costs, according to Fidelity—not including the cost of the long-term care that about three-quarters of us will need for three years on average.

How do you pay for that? If you've got liquid assets of several million or more, you can invest your money and use the earnings to fund your care. If you've got assets of under a half million, the cost of care will eat into them pretty quickly and you'll qualify for Medicaid, which does cover long-term care. But what if you're in between? Or, if you have several million or more but want to leave that money to your children rather than spend it on your care?

That's when long-term care insurance starts to make sense. It's not cheap. A single 55-year-old woman would pay about $1,000 more a year for $400,000 in total benefits than a 55-year-old man would pay. Why? Women live longer and, because we're often alone at the end of our lives, are more likely to need long-term care. That makes long-term care coverage, like disability insurance, *even more important* for single women and those without children than it is for couples and moms.

These policies are complicated, so shop carefully and with an insurance agent who specializes in the stuff. Look for companies with a strong financial strength rating and policies that include an inflation rider, and try to buy before age 60. Wait much longer and the premiums will go up or you could be rejected for health reasons. You can also consider one of the newer hybrid policies that combine a permanent life insurance policy with long-term care. If you need care, you can dip into the benefits. If you don't, they'll eventually go to your heirs.

Taking Financial Control

There may come a time when your parents can no longer manage their money themselves. Cognitive impairment may not even be a factor. If your father always handled the money and he passes away, your mother may be at a loss for what to do. You can work with her (and perhaps a financial advisor) to bring her up to speed, or you can step in and assume some financial control.

You can also preemptively avoid some problems by putting as much as you can on autopilot. After my father passed away, I tried to get my mother to pay her bills online. She was cautious and disinterested. Then she started dating Bob (who is so fully automated he often functions as in-family tech support) and jumped in with both feet. The lesson I took from this is that just like our kids may be 1,000 times more comfortable with technology than we are, we are 1,000 times more comfortable with technology than our parents. Try enlisting their most tech-savvy peers to help them get with the program.

Then, establish a financial schedule so that things work in an orderly fashion. Schedule bills to be paid directly after Social Security or pension checks clear. If credit card, utility, and other bills aren't on a convenient cycle, call the billers and ask to have this changed. If your parents want you in the loop, they can give you access so that you can monitor their accounts online and help pay the bills. Some billers will even notify you if your parents miss a payment.

Assuming your parents are okay with it, forge your own relationship with their advisors. Ask to sit in on meetings with the lawyer, accountant, and financial planner. If the plan is to use the house for money down the road, you may want the name of their real estate broker, too. Should there be a need for you to step in to a greater degree—or to assume financial control completely—you are getting into legal territory. Here are the steps to take.

- Let their advisors know what's happening. The attorney who drew up the forms (more on this in a moment) will know you have power of attorney for finances, but the financial advisor and accountant should know as well.

- Put a letter of diminished capacity in place. This is an agreement between your parent and their advisor that allows the advisor to contact the person with power of attorney if they notice cognitive decline.

- Obtain online access to accounts. Even if your parents like to receive hard copies of their bills, almost all accounts have an online option now. Use your power of attorney to establish access to their bank, brokerage, credit card, utility, and other accounts so that you can monitor what's happening if need be.

- Avoid joint accounts. Your parents may offer to put your name on their account as an alternative. Don't do it. If one of you were to get into credit trouble, the other would be impacted. Also, after death, joint assets become the sole property of the remaining owner. If you're one of a set of siblings, that could cause an inheritance squabble.

Finally, if you or your siblings are not in a position to do this yourselves, you can hire a daily money manager to pay bills, reconcile accounts, and keep your parents' financial life running. You can find one through the American Association of Daily Money Managers at AADMM.com.

The Documents Your Parents (and You) Need

Fewer than half of American adults have a formal estate plan in place, according to LexisNexis. That's a huge problem. If a parent or other older relative becomes ill or incapacitated unexpectedly, we may not have the legal authority to take care of the finances or—even worse— have a say in their care. What you're trying to avoid is a messy guardianship or conservatorship proceeding in which you have to ask a court to allow you to assume control. It's costly. It's painful. And it's avoidable. If, that is, your parents have had the following documents drawn up by an attorney (which, by the way, you should as well).

- Durable power of attorney for finances. This gives another person the ability to handle your finances on your behalf.

- Durable power of attorney for healthcare (a.k.a. a healthcare proxy or medical directive). This gives another person the ability to make health-related decisions on your behalf. A successor should be named for the person given both powers of attorney, just in case the first isn't willing or able to do the job.

- Living will. This tells a doctor/hospital of your care wishes should you become ill or incapacitated, including wishes for life support.

- HIPAA consent form. HIPAA—the Health Information Portability and Accountability Act—is responsible for keeping your health information and your parents' health information private. If your parents want you to have information about their care, they need to sign a form that allows the doctor to share it with you. The doctor's office will have the forms.

A couple of notes about these forms. Different states sometimes require different ones. If your parents (or you) spend time in a couple of states, you'll want to either make sure they have reciprocity or fill out forms for each one (if you do, make sure they're consistent). The forms don't do you any good unless someone knows they exist, either—so make a card to keep in your parents' wallets (and yes, yours) that says they exist and whom to contact. Keep copies yourself and give copies to your siblings.

Finally, encourage your parents to put together a document that is essentially a road map to follow in case of emergency. My stepfather

Bob calls this A Letter Of Instruction And Suggestion (because it can also include suggestions for how the parent hopes the child will proceed in involving siblings, caring for important causes, and otherwise living their lives). I've written one and I think you should, too. It includes the location of all the important documents (deeds, trusts, Social Security cards, birth certificates), passwords, names and phone numbers of institutions and important people to call, lists of accounts, insurance policies, safe deposit boxes, and anything else you think is truly important to running your life. Try to update it once a year.

Taking Care of You

According to the National Alliance for Caregiving, nearly 40 percent of caregivers report high emotional stress from the demands they're under. Many others, however, don't even realize the toll stress is taking. The Mayo Clinic has identified nine signs of caregiver stress, among them losing or gaining weight, not getting enough sleep (seven to nine hours a night) or getting too much, becoming easily irritated, having physical symptoms (headaches, backaches, stomach issues), or finding yourself reaching too often for alcohol or painkillers to self-soothe.

It's important to realize that where a long-term caregiving scenario is concerned, you need help. To quote Hillary Rodham Clinton: It takes a village. And, if you're caring for a parent from a distance, a small country.

"Painful. Scary. Exhausting." That's how Lisa, 50s, a rabbi and mother of three from Chicago, describes the challenge of caring for her widowed mother from nearly 800 miles away. "Difficult to be far away and to not know what to do or what is right to do." The distance is a big reason that Lisa and her younger sister (who also lives far away) made the decision to hire a geriatric care manager. The National Institute on Aging defines these people as "professional relatives." Some are nurses, others are social workers, and still others have a certification as a geriatric care manager or Aging Life Care Professional from the National

Academy of Certified Care Managers, Commission for Case Manager Certification, or the National Association of Social Workers. (Note: These certifications are important. Geriatric care managers are an unlicensed group in many states.) Geriatric care managers help map out a care plan and find the necessary specialists to help execute it. You can find one through the Aging Life Care Association at AgingLifeCare.org. Typically, you'll pay $250 to $750 for an initial assessment from one of these folks, then an hourly rate of about $150 to $200.

Lisa describes hers as a "life saver." She's a crucial piece of the village Lisa has built—but she's just one piece. Among the others she rattles off:

- The caregivers in her house
- The caregiving agency (which employs the caregivers)
- Mom's closest friends, who show up ASAP at the house or, when needed, the ER
- Mom's friends, who visit
- Lisa's friends, who are additional eyes and who listen to and support her and show up when she is there and when she is not
- A cousin, who is local and there in an emergency
- A housekeeper of thirty-plus years, who shows up to cook, visit, and check in even when she is not working
- Medical professionals who will talk to Lisa and her sister
- A pharmacy that delivers
- The electrician, handyman, and plumber who can be counted on in a pinch
- And, of course, Lisa's sister ("I couldn't do this alone," she says)

There is also a family friend who has, for years, advised Lisa's parents on their investments. Every month, he reviews her mom's finances, tweaks the investments if necessary, and—Lisa says, "tells [her] what to do." The one thing Lisa is not worried about, thankfully, is money. Her parents saved and invested and made wise decisions. But that doesn't mean managing the finances isn't an arduous process. "When I visit, I review the bills she has paid, review her investments and bank account statements, and file her papers. I help her gather papers for her accountant. I work on her investments with our family friend. And I regularly explain to my mother what she has."

There are a few ways Lisa is fortunate. Her mother still lives in the home—and the community—in which Lisa was raised. The doctors, lawyers, accountants, and other advisors are not strangers. If you don't know the professionals—or neighbors—in your parent's life, now is the time to introduce yourself to them. Do the same with housekeepers, dog walkers, or other regular service providers. And before you bring anyone who will be spending time with your parent into a home, check their references and into their background. Google their name and the keyword *care* or *caregiver*. Look for online reviews on sites like Care.com. If you have the resources, consider hiring someone from the National Association of Professional Background Screeners at napbs.com to conduct a check. And don't stop there, Care.com's Sheila Marcelo says. "I'm a big believer in auditing, surprise visits, checking in and making sure that this caregiver is a fit." She's also supportive of nanny cams—as long as you're transparent with your caregiver—especially with dependents like seniors who you may know have dementia or Alzheimer's and are not able to communicate regularly or well.

One final note about managing this village you're building. Clarity is key. You need to be specific about what you need done, when you need it done, and—in many cases—how you want it done, says eldercare attorney Nicole Wipp. This is true of both professionals and friends who are pitching in. "We can't expect people to read our minds or to know on a day-to-day basis what needs to be done, or what would help us the most personally," she says. "If you don't tell someone what you want them to do, they're just going to come and do what they think you need; half the time it's not what you wanted."

And a Comfortable Place to Live

The vast majority of baby boomers want to grow old exactly where they are rather than moving to a place specifically designed to help with aging. This is what we call aging in place. Your parents start out living independently but bring in caregivers and other helpers when needed.

What adult children want is often very different. "The natural inclination for an adult child is to immediately say that the parent should move closer to me so I can take care of them," says gerontologist Mary Jo Saavedra. "The problem there—before you even get into housing—is that you've removed them from their social structure. Isolation is as deadly as smoking fifteen cigarettes a day or being obese. Having that connection and meaning in your life is very important to thrive as a human being." And that's not all. With all good intentions, you may have taken them away from their doctors, their activities, their routines.

So ask the questions: Where do you want to live? Do you have the resources to do it?

Answer 1: If they want to stay…

Look closely at their home to see if it needs to be physically altered. A 2014 report from Harvard's Joint Center for Housing Studies cites five features a home must have to make it suitable for aging: A no-step entry, single-floor living, doorways that are thirty-six inches wide (with hallways forty-two inches wide to accommodate wheelchairs), accessible electrical switches and controls, and lever-style doors and faucet handles. Only 1 percent of the homes in the US have them all.

Getting them, of course, costs money. If your parents need money to renovate—or for other reasons—the idea of a reverse mortgage may come up. Reverse mortgages, which allow people to borrow the equity from their home while continuing to live there, are complicated and pricey. But there are some situations in which they work.

The interest rates on these loans are fixed (which is a good thing) and borrowers can access the money as a lump sum, in monthly increments (i.e., like a paycheck), or as a line of credit on which you pay interest only on the amount you borrow. This last option is the most attractive because it allows borrowers to use a reverse mortgage like a home equity line of credit you have just for emergencies. In years when stocks have tumbled and your parents don't want to sell assets in their retirement portfolios (because they think they'll eventually rebound), they can pull money from their home to live on instead. Then, when the markets do rebound, they can repay the reverse mortgage and go back to using money from retirement accounts.

The commercials tout that these loans don't have to be repaid until the homeowner dies or is living elsewhere for at least a year. That's true, but the downside to a reverse mortgage is that when money has been borrowed from the home, interest will accrue. That interest eats into the money your parents (or you) receive if and when the home is sold. They (or you) can walk away with zero. If they ever needed to move to an assisted living facility or nursing home, that cash would have come in handy.

Answer 2: If they want to go...

That puts more options on the plate. One is downsizing, or moving into a home better equipped to handle aging. Another is moving into a community specifically designed for aging, an assisted living or continuing care retirement community (CCRC). While some of these are basic, others have as many activities and amenities as a cruise ship. When adults move in, they typically live on their own. As they need additional care, they can move into assisted living, and eventually—if need be—into the nursing part of the facility, where care is available around the clock.

Dana, the solar power entrepreneur from California, explains that for many years her parents refused to even consider assisted living, then decided to explore CCRCs. And they fell head over heels. "They feel like they're moving into a resort," she says. "My dad can get his hair cut.

There are lots of activities." The price tag, however, is high. The financial application started with a credit check and a deep dive into the couple's net worth. The contract Dana's parents signed stipulates that they have to sell their home and that the CCRC has a first call on all of their assets. "We finally got it in writing that they don't kick anyone out for running out of money," Dana says. "But they don't accept you unless they think it makes financial sense."

That's fairly typical. Entering a CCRC often entails a deposit (sometimes called a buy-in) of between $100,000 and $1 million, with an average of about $250,000. This money is the facility's insurance against the care your parents might need in the future. Then there are monthly costs, which start at a few thousand and go up from there. All of this will be laid out in the contract you sign. Make sure a lawyer reads it before your parents—or anyone else in your family—sign.

And then there's my mom, who has suggested she'd prefer to live with me and my husband rather than any sort of assisted living facility—a suggestion that is actually quite trendy. According to AARP, the number of parents moving in with their grown kids has spiked in recent years. There are many things to consider before you make a move like this, including space, whether your home will need to be renovated to work for your parent, and what sorts of services you'll need to bring in so that you can continue to work (if that's the plan). You may even decide, as we have, that maybe your parents shouldn't move—but you should.

My husband and I have recently been exploring a move to Center City, Philadelphia, which is where my mom lives. As you might expect, my mother is worried about this. She is worried that I won't have enough friends and that it will be too difficult for me to commute to New York City a couple of days a week for work. Mostly, she is horrified that this is all about her. It's not. It's about taxes. And property values. And proximity to the beach community we go to in the summer. And the fact that there's lots of family nearby. But, yes, it's about her, too. We'll keep talking so that we can both get comfortable with that.

What Have We Learned

- *Caregivers look a lot like you (today, or perhaps in the future). They're women with careers and kids of their own who make room for what is essentially an additional full-time job: taking care of Mom and Dad. The goal is to do so without damaging your own financial future. If hiring a caregiver is equivalent to your salary, hire the caregiver so that you can maintain your income growth.*

- *We're a lot more prepared to do this if we've had ongoing conversations about our parents' existing resources so that we understand what we and our siblings need to provide, and then clearing the financial and legal hurdles that allow us to do it.*

- *As you care for your parents, don't forget about yourself. You need the same wills, powers of attorney, and other documents as they do. And the right time to purchase long-term care insurance (if you're going to buy it at all) is around age 50.*

Where Do We Go from Here

One of the big advantages of being a woman with money is that it gives us leeway not just to create a legacy for our children and families, but to make an impact on the world around us. Here's how to think about that.

⌣

CHAPTER 12

Leaving a Legacy

*My husband always had in his head the dollar amount
that would allow us to maintain our standard of living
throughout our projected life. By the time I was 49 and he was
51, we'd already hit that number. So we started talking about
what happens now? Should we retire just because we have
enough money? Theoretically on paper, we would. But we're
both at a stage where we're enjoying what we're doing. So we
[decided to continue to keep working]. If, in the grand scheme
of things, it means we can make contributions to charities that
matter to us in a bigger way, I get excited about that. I feel like
wealth in the right hands can change the world.*
—Lisa, 50s, health and wellness entrepreneur, Wisconsin

~

I say: *Amen to that.* Which happens to be a very female reaction.
Neuroscientists from the University of Zurich compared male and
female brains in the process of making decisions about giving. What
they saw (you can see the brain in action using MRIs) was that female
brains had stronger reactions to generous impulses (giving to others)
while male brains reacted more strongly to selfish ones (doing things
for themselves). The researchers, whose findings were chronicled in
ScienceDaily in 2017, noted that there may be a little question of nature
versus nurture here. Other studies have shown that girls (more than boys)
are encouraged to be generous and are praised when we are. The activity

...ur brains may be a learned response rather than one we're born with. Either way, the urge to give back—to leave our mark on our kids, communities, the world—is something we feel. And many of us feel it deeply.

What Does It Mean to Leave a Legacy?

Legacy is, simultaneously, one of the most vague and most intimidating words in the English language. Legacies are children who are expected to get into Ivy League schools because their parents went there before them. They're obsolete versions of computer software. But most often, we think of them as what's left behind by exceptionally wealthy, powerful people after death.

Here's a better definition: Your legacy is the difference you want to make in the lives of other people. It's a gift—sometimes money, others not—and you don't have to be dead to pass it along.

In fact, waiting until death is wasting opportunity, says Susan Turnbull, founder of Personal Legacy Advisors. Thinking about your legacy and what you want it to be means thinking about what kind of an influence you want to be on your world and in your circle. Answering these questions is not just the first step in estate planning for the future. It can also provide guidance while you're living your life.

This is one of those financial planning challenges that's both emotional and tactical. It involves thinking about: What impact do you want to make? (Do you want to help stop hunger? Gun violence? Do you want to raise the next generation of compassionate humans? Or ready a particular woman or two to rise to the C-suite?) Whom do you want to make that impact on? (Your own kids? Your community? Victims of a disease that has claimed members of your family? Residents of a country far away?) When do you want to have this effect? (Now? Later? Now and later?) How are you going to move the needle? (By giving money? Volunteering? Mentoring? Parenting in a particular way?)

The point is: It's your choice.

- Christine, 30s, a business coach in Kentucky, had a daughter who was stillborn. She and her husband started a nonprofit organization to help other families survive similar tragedies. She says: *I want to help other people know it's not only possible to survive but to thrive after going through something so life-alteringly traumatic.*

- Diane, 60s, a retired school district superintendent in New Jersey, is determined that her beach house at the Jersey Shore, already in the family for several generations, will flow to the next without a hitch. She says: *We've made it so that our son won't have to pay for anything but taxes and incidentals. The house is our family legacy. It was my grandparents' house. That's a core of our family. I want to provide security so it won't be a financial burden to him or his kids.*

- Jenn, 30s, a commercial banker from Tennessee, says she "loves money"—not just because it keeps her family of four more than comfortable but because it empowers her to do good for others. She says: *We very much live below our means and like to donate and help in as many different ways as we can. For me, accumulating wealth is just an ability to pass it on. We can't take any of it with us. I hope and pray that my children are financially stable so they don't need my money and our wealth can go to help many other people.*

Preparing Your Kids

In Chapter 10 we talked about raising kids to value the wonderful life you provide for them—and respect the hard work and money that it takes to do so. In some ways, that's all preparation for what happens down the road when you pass away and they inherit some or all of what you've left behind. We've all heard stories of inheritances gone wrong or mismanaged. Amy Castoro, president of the Williams Group, which advises wealthy families, says it's the rule rather than the exception. Research conducted by her firm found that 70 percent of families lose their wealth when it transitions from one generation to the next. When they looked at why that happened, 60 percent of the time it was a breakdown in communication or trust, 25 percent was due to heirs not being prepared, and 10 percent of the time it was because the family members disagreed about their basic values.

Often it's not just the money that's lost—it's the relationships between siblings and other family members as well. "The saddest story is when kids inherit money and they have no direction," she says. "They get swallowed up by their life of affluence and they lose sight of what's important." And, no, it doesn't have to be millions of dollars. Castoro says she's seen families break apart over $150,000. "How much money you have doesn't matter," she insists.

Again, preparation starts with conversation—not just one, but a series over their lifetimes. If you are going to leave money to your children—or plan on giving to them while you are alive (more on that in a moment), they should, at some point, be aware of it so that they can figure it into their own financial planning. If, for example, you plan on contributing to college for your grandchildren or leaving money for that purpose if you're no longer around, letting your children know that allows them to prioritize their own retirement and not worry so much about funding 529s. If you think your children believe they will be inheriting more than they actually will, managing their expectations is equally important. They may not be saving enough because they're so secure in the belief that there will be a windfall. And, if you're not sure what will be left because you're concerned about your own extended life span—and funding the cost of your own care—you'll want to express that as well. The point is to give them a picture of their financial future that is in line with reality.

These conversations also offer an opportunity for you to pass along values and expectations for how at least some of the money will be used. My parents both graduated from Temple University in Philadelphia. They were incredibly grateful to the place, mostly for helping my father find his way, then setting him on a course he'd follow for the rest of his life. About fifteen years ago now—a few years before my father passed away—my parents gave the university $25,000 to endow a lecture series. (I tell you the amount because I want you to know that you don't have to have Warren Buffett money to make a difference.) Since then, it has grown—through good management and additional contributions—to over $100,000 and it's now a scholarship fund, providing a third of the annual funding each year for a student majoring in communications, like my dad. I will give money to that fund every year for the rest of my life. I may leave something for it in my will. And I expect my brothers will do the same. Why? Not just because it has our family's name on it—but because our parents talked with us about *why* they were doing this and how strongly they felt about supporting Temple (which still provides a valuable educational home for city kids, like they were, who may not otherwise be able to afford college). By talking about it, our parents made it clear this was not just *their* thing, this was a *family* thing.

These conversations also offer opportunities for your kids to weigh in and tell you what they want and what they value. The key, says wealth advisor Amy Castoro, is—through years of practice—giving them the skills to be able to say, "Even though I was born first, that doesn't mean I want to run the family business." Or, "I know you support cancer research and I value that, but green energy is also important to me. Could we point some of our giving in that direction."

FAIR VS. EQUAL

About one-third of parents don't leave money equally to their heirs. That was the finding from a 2015 paper from the National Bureau of Economic Research, and frankly, the number is a lot higher than I would have expected. Why? Because, particularly to siblings, not being left equal amounts of money (or whatever) can feel like a bee sting, which is bad enough. But not *knowing* that an estate will be distributed unequally? That's a hornet's nest. "You've got to talk to your kids," says estate planning attorney Les Kotzer. "They won't work it out after you die. They'll work it out with their lawyers."

And yet there are perfectly valid reasons why you may want to leave unequal bequests to your kids or other heirs. Need is a big one. Special needs children often require more in the way of support than other children. But there are other scenarios where some children are much more successful than others. "There are three sons in the Manning family, there's Eli, Peyton, and the third one, Cooper," says New York estate planning attorney Lawrence Mandelker. "Are the Manning parents being unfair if they leave more property to the third son, the one who didn't sign multimillion-dollar contracts to play in the NFL?" Living arrangements may also lead to unequal distribution of your assets. If one of your children is living with you later in life, taking you to the dentist and doctor and otherwise taking care of you, it might be understandable that you'd leave her the house. Family businesses are another common example. When one child works in the business but another doesn't, should they still inherit equal shares? And what about the scenario where you paid $200,000 for graduate school for one child when the others didn't go? Do you have to level the playing field later on?

Equal isn't always fair. Fair isn't always equal. But you must, must, must telegraph your intentions with the understanding of the fact that kids keep mental records of who got what, when during life. If you plan on leaving some of your money to charity, you should let your kids in on that as well.

"When you're watching a football game, as long as there's a referee, it's okay," says Kotzer. "Imagine a football game without a referee. The parent, in this case, is the referee." If you want the game to continue after you're gone, it's your job to establish the rules.

To Wait or Not to Wait?

A long time ago, for reasons that aren't relevant here, I purchased a whole life insurance policy. I was thinking about it recently—deciding whether to maintain it or let it lapse—when it struck me. If I live until I'm 100 (which seems to be getting likelier every day) my kids won't see that money until they're in their 70s. What good will it do them then? Well, I thought, maybe some. It could help them pay for the fact that they'll likely live to be 110. But perhaps they could use at least some of it earlier—to help with down payments for homes that seem harder to attain every day, to put their own kids (the grandkids I imagine I'll have someday) through college, or to start a business.

If there's any question that you might need the money you've amassed before you pass away, holding off on distributing it makes sense. But, if you're certain that you can afford it, giving while you're alive allows your heirs to check off some of their life goals—and allows you to enjoy seeing them doing it. You can give up to $15,000 (in 2019, the numbers go up over time) a year to as many individuals as you want tax-free; they don't have to pay taxes for receiving it and you don't have to pay taxes for making the gift. If you're married, you and your spouse can each give $15,000—or a combined $30,000—to the same individuals. And—a little quick math—if your child has a significant other and you're trying to help them buy a house, you and your spouse can each move $15,000 a year to each of them, which could provide a nice, tidy tax-free $60,000 to help them on their way.

Your children aren't the only ones who can be on the receiving end of your generosity. Sharon, the Portland CEO, wants to give her nieces and nephews a leg up when they need it rather than waiting until she passes away. She's put aside money to enable them to go to college without taking on student loans and to help with the down payments on their first homes. "I feel that I'm the last and best shot [they have]," she says.

Again, you want to be very clear about what you're doing, why you're doing it, and—importantly—how often you plan on doing it. If you start a pattern of giving your kids an annual $15,000, they will quickly come to rely on that money. Don't do it habitually unless you're certain you will be able to continue. Likewise, if it's a onetime thing, let them know that as well.

The Basic Documents

Figuring out what you want to do with your money is step one. Making it happen comes next—and that involves legal documents. According to a 2017 survey from Caring.com, only 42 percent of American adults—and only 36 percent of those with young children—have an end-of-life plan, including a will, in place.

Very few things upset me more than hearing about parents of young kids who don't have wills. A will is *the only* document that allows you to name guardians for those kids. Without one, the court gets to decide—via an arduous and often messy process called a guardianship proceeding—who gets them, and the result may not be the person you would have chosen. If you're reading this and feeling guilty because you're one of those parents, put the book down *right now* and make an appointment with a lawyer to draw up a will. When you're back, I'll explain what else you need.

The irony of the big and intimidating process known as estate planning is that even if you don't do it, you've done it, Mandelker explains. If you've bought an insurance policy and named a beneficiary, you've done estate planning. If you named a joint owner to a bank account (not always a good idea, see page 213), you've done estate planning. Anything you own is governed by property laws, so when you die, that property is going to pass either according to those laws—or according to things you've put in place to bypass those laws.

If you die intestate—i.e., without a will—the state stipulates what happens to your property. In New York, for example, if you're married with no kids, everything goes to the spouse. If you're married with kids, the first $50,000 goes to your spouse and the rest gets split. The spouse gets half and the kids get half. The problem with this, Mandelker notes, is that it's the same for everyone and doesn't take your specific circumstances into account. "You could be in the midst of a divorce," he says. "It doesn't matter. [In the eyes of the law] you're still married. You could have one child with whom you haven't spoken in ten years, but they are still going to get the same share as the child that lives with you."

If you don't want things done that way, you need to use a will to explain how you want it done instead. And there are some assets for which wills don't have the final say—including retirement accounts (which go to your spouse unless a spouse signs a letter disclaiming them), and assets that are put in trusts.

So what do you need? The same basic documents we outlined for your parents on page 214: a will, living will, healthcare proxy, and durable power of attorney for finances. For many people, that's enough. But if you're looking to either avoid probate, avoid estate taxes, or attach strings to the gifts you're giving, it's not.

Let's dispense with the probate issue first. You've probably heard of a very common type of trust called a living trust—which lawyers tend to call a "revocable trust" because a) that's the technical term and b) you know, they're lawyers. You establish this while you're alive, transfer ownership of assets into it, and, typically, direct your will to move any remaining assets into it when you die. Also, *revocable* means it can be undone or changed. With irrevocable trusts, once you put assets into them, they're no longer yours. Assets that are in a living trust don't have to go through probate, so they can be dealt with immediately rather than waiting for the state to prove the will is valid. So do you need one? If you own property in more than one state, probate can be a hassle, so living trusts offer an advantage. If you're concerned about privacy, living trusts have an edge—they're private; wills are not. But, as they tend to be more expensive to prepare than wills, they also have a history of being oversold. Don't let yourself be talked into one if you don't need it.

Now, on to estate taxes. The 2017 tax law raised the amount of money each individual can pass on to heirs tax-free to about $11.2 million. Married couples can pass on double that. The law resets to the old limits (roughly $5.5 million for individuals, $11 million for couples) in 2025 if Congress doesn't extend it. Either way, it's a lot of money. If you have $5 million or more in assets—and you don't want your heirs to pay taxes for receiving it, it's time to see an estate planning attorney. (In fact, at this level of assets, you should see one even if you're not worried about taxes.) At a minimum, if you're married you're going to want to talk about preserving each person's individual ability to pass along up to $11 million plus in assets tax-free, which means setting up something called a "marital" or "bypass" trust. (Complications ensue if this trust isn't in place when the first spouse dies, because everything then flows to the surviving spouse. If as a result the survivor winds up with more money than can be passed along tax-free, the ultimate heirs may owe taxes on the family money. Time to lawyer up.)

Marital/bypass trusts are among the simplest ones on the menu of legal documents that reads like something out of the Deep South, with GRITs and GRATs and GRUTs taking center stage. I am not going to explain the minutiae of all of these documents, which, unlike unicorns, *are* real. But I will explain the point: Death, like life, has an annoying habit of not always happening when you expect it. You don't want to put your heirs in the position of having assets that they're not equipped to handle. Trusts, which you can think of as gifts with strings attached (usually in a good way), can help. They're essentially holding pens for all types of assets—cash, securities, real estate, life insurance. The giver either puts assets into trust or directs the estate to do so at death (this is called a testamentary trust). The trust is managed by someone chosen by the giver (the trustee), and the assets (the income and the principal) are doled out to the beneficiaries either as instructed or at the trustee's discretion.

A woman at the HerMoney Happy Hour outside San Francisco noted that she'd been helped by a trust like that. "I went to private school, paid for by a trust set up by my grandparents," she said. "My kids' tuition is paid for by a trust set up by my in-laws. There are a lot of benefits to doing it that way—tuition can be bigger than a mortgage. If we—hopefully—have grandchildren and money, I will try to do that for them."

Whether the money is passing from parents to children, from grandparents, or from a long history of family money, estate planning attorneys use different strategies to ensure that kids come into their wealth *slowly*. A 21-year-old coming into a $1 million life insurance payout all at once might think they're rich and not finish college—or make some other reckless move—as a result. Instead, we dole out the money piecemeal—a chunk might become available at age 25 when they're finishing up their education, another at 30 when they marry and buy a house, another at 35 when they have children. The hope is that even if they blow the first installment (because, you know, brains—especially male ones—aren't fully cooked until the mid 20s) they'll have wised up when they come into the latter two. Other estate planners recommend "lifetime trusts," where assets don't automatically get pushed out of trusts at particular ages but instead stay in until they're needed for health, education, or even discretionary reasons (you set the terms in advance). The benefit of the latter is that if your child has a creditor issue or is going through a divorce right about the time they're due to come into a chunk of money, those assets can remain in the protection of the trust.

Another important protection play is to choose the trustee (or trustees) wisely, then empower that person (or persons) to make other payments in a scenario that would line up with your values. In the case of marital trusts (which would be put in place for the benefit of you or your spouse), the assets of the spouse who dies first typically go into trust to be used for the benefit of the surviving spouse. Because this is typically a case of using a trust for protection from taxes rather than protection from adolescent impulses, you want to name someone who has a good relationship with the surviving spouse and give them a relatively free hand to distribute not just income on the trust but principal if needed.

When the trust is for the benefit of children, you need to be more careful to choose someone who won't roll over when the kids ask for money for purposes that might not be in their best long-term interests. The other benefit of putting money in trust is creditor protection. If your child, in this instance, owes money to a credit card company, to a divorcing spouse, or because of a lawsuit, the creditor can't touch anything in the trust.

Trusts can also be set up with incentives attached, where the gifts aren't made until the recipients clear hurdles that the trust specifies. A trust can be written to pay a sum on graduation from college. If they go through law school and pass the bar, you might direct the trust to give them more. Experts are mixed on whether these are a good idea that can help pass values from generation to generation or a pretty horrible one. "Incentives based on education, degrees attained, and salary earned can be problematic because they can fail to properly reflect your intentions," says Mandelker. "Do you want to penalize your child because they went into social work rather than going to a hedge fund?"

I'm not a fan. I was raised by parents whose admonishment to "do what you think is right" was enough to get me to keep curfew (most of the time) and steer clear of the smokers at the back of the high school. I was also that kind of kid. But just like I don't believe in paying kids for grades, I don't think this is a long-term solution. Too often what you wind up with is a miserable adult who goes down a road chosen for her, then spends too much of that inheritance griping about it on the therapist's couch.

An alternative is what's called an ethical will, which you can write yourself. This nonlegal document with Jewish roots is essentially a letter in which you put into writing your wishes for how your children and grandchildren move forward in their lives—and put your assets to use. "It's an opportunity for people to create an enduring expression of what's important to them," says advisor Susan Turnbull. For some people, it begins and ends with expressions of love and gratitude. For others, it's a way to communicate information: Here's why I decided to set up my estate the way I did. These are the motivations behind my charitable choices. This is what's important for you to know about our heritage. And—sometimes—it's used to tidy up unfinished business in a family. You can pass it along during life or leave it with your other papers to be accessed when you die. You may even want to put it in video form. The whole idea, says Turnbull, is to pass along the point that "our wealth is so much more than our money." I like the sound of that.

Change the World by Giving Money Away

I have to admit, it first sounded a little funny to my ears when my kids—describing their fund-raising activities at college—referred to it as their "philanthropy." But they were, they *are*, right. Just as you don't need millions to leave a legacy—there's no measure of wealth that creates a philanthropist. Anyone who donates money, time, talent, or skills in pursuit of a better world falls into the category. And just like we want to make the most of the money we're leaving to our children or other heirs, we should want to maximize the benefit our gifts can have to the causes we support.

Sure, there are times you show up for your friend's gala (or serve on the committee or chair it) because you love her, or because she did that for you. (As my friend Jonathan once wrote on an invitation to a fund-raiser for his favorite nonprofit: "This is the price of friendship." Touché.) But there are other opportunities to be more thoughtful, more planned in how we allocate the resources we put aside for charity. Many of us don't take advantage of them—we're responsive in our giving rather than proactive.

The result is that we end up feeling a little underwhelmed. "I would love to say I can use my money to make a difference, but I don't always feel I have the money to make a big impact," says Julie, 30s, the reading specialist from Pennsylvania. "I donate small amounts to charities and support friends and families in the fund-raising efforts for various causes. I always try to contribute what I can, but I never walk away feeling like my donation in particular has made a difference."

I understand the sentiment. When the charitable headlines feature billionaires pledging to give away half their worth, it's pretty easy to feel insignificant. But all you have to do is look at the success of the Ice Bucket Challenge—which raised over $100 million and funded research that ultimately identified a new gene, which could lead to treatment of ALS—or the millions of small donations pooled together that made Bernie Sanders a viable candidate in the 2018 election to know that small individual gifts matter.

Especially when they're made by women. Because women are going to own an estimated 70 percent of North American GDP, *we* are going to be the ones changing the landscape of charitable giving, explains advisor Gena Rotstein. Charities aren't uniformly excited about this. When men make a gift of $10,000 or more, they usually make that decision within six months; women take an average of three years. We are also going to be influencing the way charitable organizations will be designed, structured, and managed.

It's best to be proactive about our giving. Rather than writing checks in reaction to outreach from others, we need to flip the script. Being methodical and strategic about your charitable contributions can make sure that you're getting the most bang for your philanthropic dollar. That means:

Knowing what you're trying to accomplish—and how much you're devoting to the effort. To be more planned about your giving, you need a handle on two pieces of information: What change are you looking to make? And how much in the way of resources do you have to devote to doing it? Both are completely up to you, but by identifying what the changes are and the money or time you're committing, you have two points of data by which to evaluate your success. That's what Eliana, the New York attorney in her 30s, and her husband have done. "We have a spreadsheet of all the organizations that we want to support and a set amount of money each year that we are able to donate, which we divide among these organizations," she says. "We try to raise the total amount we donate every year and add and subtract organizations from our list all the time." Once you've got this sort of plan in place, it's easier to tell organizations that reach out to you that your money is already committed, *because it is.* You may also want to set aside a small pot of discretionary money for when your friends ask. That way you can stick to your mission without feeling like Grinch central.

Giving more to fewer causes. Because of the overhead that charities must spend to process each donation, giving larger donations to a smaller number of places ensures that they get more of each dollar. One way to accomplish this is to set up a recurring donation—a monthly or quarterly gift that you commit to and that is automatically drafted from your bank account or billed to your credit card. This allows the charity to operate more efficiently. They know they can count on your gift so they can spend less money reaching out to you, explains Shannon McCracken, chief development officer at Charity Navigator. It also helps smooth their cash flows. "So much money comes in December," she says. "But they need to spend money all year round."

Doing your research. The last decade has seen the rise of impact philanthropy, which—in addition to focusing on social impact—aims to help givers find opportunities to make the biggest difference with their dollars (rather than, say, honoring the memory of a loved one). If that is of interest, resources from the Center for High Impact Philanthropy at the University of Pennsylvania (impact.upenn.edu) can point you in the right direction. At a minimum, check websites like GuideStar and Charity Navigator to figure out how your donations will be spent.

And getting the most from your gifts in return—during life and at death. Two principles govern the strategy here. First, as long as you're itemizing (even under the new tax law), charitable contributions are deductible. And second, because charities don't pay taxes on capital gains, it pays to choose carefully which assets you give to charity. If you give inflated assets (like stocks) to a charity, the charity doesn't have to pay taxes upon selling them whereas you would. That allows you to essentially give away more for less. A good estate planning attorney can help you with this part of your legacy as well. Among the strategies to consider:

- Making the charity the beneficiary of a particular asset or account. This can be a smart tax move, particularly for tax-deferred accounts like an IRA or 401(k), since charities won't have to pay income taxes on it but heirs would. To reduce the amount of taxes, you'd leave some or all of the retirement accounts to charity, while passing along other assets that don't come with a tax burden to your heirs.

- Opening a donor-advised fund account. This is something you'd do during life. You make contributions—of cash, stock, real estate, or other assets—into this account as you like and take a tax deduction each time you do (again, assuming you itemize). The fund invests the assets and they grow tax-free. Then you make contributions out of the fund to qualified charities, or your heirs do so when you die.

- Putting assets in a charitable remainder trust. These are irrevocable trusts—meaning once you put the money or assets into them, you can't get them back. You make a contribution (again, pretty much any asset will do) into the trust and get a tax benefit for doing so. The assets in the trust are invested and you (or your heirs) can receive an income stream from those investments for a set period of years. When the trust expires, the charitable beneficiary receives the money that remains.

- Putting assets into a charitable lead trust. Same idea, but in reverse. The income from the trust is distributed to the charity for a set number of years. Once the term expires, the remaining assets go to your heirs. (Note: There are a lot of permutations on charitable trusts. If these sound interesting, talk to a lawyer.)

- Setting up a charitable gift annuity. You make a gift to a charity today, get a partial tax write-off on the amount, and the charity pays you an income stream on that gift for the rest of your life. When you die, the charity keeps what's left.

Doing Well by Doing Good

In early 2018, Larry Fink, the chairman of BlackRock, the world's largest investment company, signaled his firm would be more actively pushing the companies it invests in to consider the broader impact of their business decisions. "Society is demanding that companies, both public and private, serve a social purpose," he wrote in the annual BlackRock letter to CEOs. "To prosper over time, every company must not only deliver financial performance, but also show how it makes a positive contribution to society. Companies must benefit all of their stakeholders, including shareholders, employees, customers, and the communities in which they operate."

You don't have to give money away to do good in the world—you can also create change by investing it. *Impact investing* is putting money to work to create a measurable, beneficial social or environmental change—while providing a competitive return on your money at the same time.

A couple of decades ago, we had socially responsible investing. It was organized around negatives—not investing in the stocks of tobacco or gun manufacturers, not buying mutual funds that had those businesses in their portfolios. Making money by investing this way was more of an afterthought.

Impact investing is more like *Moneyball*. Rather than screening for things that companies are doing wrong, it involves screening for those that are doing things right in three basic categories the industry calls ESG: environmental (like water use, sustainable resources, and climate change), social (including avoiding tobacco and focusing on workplace benefits, diversity and anti-bias, and human rights), and corporate governance (for example, board diversity and board independence). And it's growing fast. According to the Forum for Sustainable and Responsible Investment, by the end of 2015 more than $1 out of every $5 under professional management in the US was invested by these principles. Women and millennials are leading the way.

"When I need to purchase something, whether it's a car or tires for my car, I'll do a lot of research and try to get all the information I need to make the best possible decision. I use the facts to narrow down my choices but if it doesn't make me feel good emotionally, I won't buy it," says Elissa, 40s, a management consultant from Ohio. She feels the same about her investments. "I do the research before I decide, is that a good stock to buy or not? Do I like what the company does? Do I feel good about putting this amount of money into this stock?"

Today, there are well over one hundred ESG funds, including index funds and ETFs. Google them and you'll see that some are broad "social" indexes while others focus on gender diversity or clean energy, or being fossil fuel free. And, although we don't have as many years of performance history on them as we do on the markets as a whole (particularly in down markets), investing this way doesn't appear to drag down returns. Some research indicates it may do the opposite. The Morgan Stanley Institute for Sustainable Investing reviewed performance data from 2008 to 2014 and found that ESG funds tend to be less volatile and produce higher returns. Why would this be the case? Look back to those ESG principles. It's not hard to see that companies that offer good workplace benefits would translate to happier, more productive workers, which could benefit the bottom line and the stock price.

ESG screening can also spot problems in companies before they happen. Nuveen Investments' Martin Kremenstein, who has launched a series of funds driven by ESG criteria, explained that screening for these positive factors led his company to remove Volkswagen from its portfolio before its emissions scandal and Equifax from its portfolio before the data breach. How did the screens see those problems coming? They didn't *precisely*. But they did have overall data security concerns about Equifax and environmental control concerns about VW. Kremenstein explains: "When you look at what we're scoring on: Do you use your resources efficiently? Do you treat your staff well? Do you treat your customers well? All of those are non-financial quality factors [that give you a better sense of the company]."

The biggest hurdle for wannabe impact investors has been a shortage of places to put their money. Building any diverse portfolio typically includes investments in large, global companies, and these are the sort that may be eliminated by ESG screens. The solution Kremenstein and others have come to is to eliminate the companies doing business in the traditional "sin sectors" (tobacco, alcohol, firearms, and nuclear) and then pick the best in class from the rest of the companies in the universe and include them in the portfolio. That allows energy and utility companies to remain. "You end up with a portfolio with a desire to do good," he says. "A market portfolio that reduces that carbon footprint as well."

Changing the World in Other Ways

Finally, it's important to note that there are other ways you can use your money to create change in the world around you. It's not just about sharing it or investing it, being thoughtful about how you earn it (perhaps choosing to work for a nonprofit or an organization that shares your overall values) and spend it can also have a significant impact. As I was putting the finishing touches on this chapter, Laura Ingraham of Fox News used Twitter to criticize a teenage survivor of the shooting at Marjory Stoneman Douglas High School in Parkland, Florida. The student turned to social media himself and rallied advertisers to boycott Ingraham's show.

The advertisers weren't scared of high school senior David Hogg. They were frightened that you would see logic in his remarks, see them on Ingraham's show, and stop buying their products. "With money you're voting every single day," says Nathan Dungan, founder and president of Share Save Spend, a company aimed at helping individuals and families align their financial decisions with their values. "When you start to total up those votes, it's a lot of votes. And if you have lots of people talking about their votes, that's a lot of power, and then all of a sudden you're changing the world."

It's an idea that's gaining steam. According to a report from Cone Communications, 87 percent of consumers will purchase a product because a company advocated for an issue they cared about, and 76 percent refuse to purchase a company's products or services upon learning it supported an issue contrary to their beliefs.

It's easy to get overwhelmed if you start thinking about or trying to research the business practices and supply chain of every single product that you purchase. But if there are a few issues that you feel strongly about (supporting animal rights and local businesses, reducing waste), making some changes to the way that you shop could ensure that your money isn't going to support practices to which you're opposed. That can make you feel better overall about your spending. And that is never a bad thing.

What Have We Learned

- *With more money in the hands of women, we can make more of an impact—on our families and communities, but also on the world at large.*

- *Crafting your legacy means being thoughtful about the various ways you give money away while you're alive and at death. Where children, in particular, are concerned, trusts are a useful vehicle to make sure they don't come into too much money before they're ready to handle it.*

- *You can also make an impact on the world by the way you both invest and spend. And you don't have to give up returns on your money or quality in the products you buy in order to do it.*

Afterword: The Big Takeaway
(or What Have We Learned Overall)

A confession: When I started writing the summaries at the end of each chapter, I struggled with the heading to give them. Was "What Have We Learned" too earnest? Too didactic? But then I realized how much *I* had learned—from the women at my happy hours, the podcast listeners who wrote in, and the experts interviewed for this project. And, I decided, it was just right. As women, our financial power—and our power in the world—is growing at such a fast clip, we have to keep learning to simply keep up with it. And so here's what I hope you take away as you come to the end of these pages.

From Part I

Your relationship with money—why you use it, react to it, think about it in the way you as an individual do—depends on the things in life that propel you to reach for them. Whether you're driven by security, power, independence, the urge to do good in the world, or something else entirely has a lot to do with both the way you were raised (you may be in a totally different sphere now, but it's tough to escape) and how all of us, as humans, are wired. But understanding these things, and the way they impact not just us but also how we function with our partners, families, and friends, is a key building block toward getting a financial grip.

From Part II

Once we've got our money selves tamed (or at least understood), we can begin to maximize the financial power we already have—and make moves to gain even more. Yes, Time's Up when it comes to closing the gender wage gap in this country, but that's a tall order. So, let's focus on closing it one woman at a time by advocating for our own pay and making sure the women we employ are paid fairly. And earning money by working is just step one. It's time to take our seats at the investment table. This doesn't mean we're trading individual stocks every day, but rather that we're paying attention to the money we have working for us in our retirement (and other) accounts and making sure it's on track to accomplish our goals. Investing in our own businesses and in homes we live in (or rent out for income) are other important ways to bring in more money. And then, yes, we need to give ourselves permission to *enjoy* the benefits all this hard work brings. *Spending* is not a dirty word. We should do it in ways that make us feel good.

From Part III

Once we've got ourselves conquered we can move on to the other important people in our lives—and in the world. As women, we spend a great deal of time and energy focused on our kids, our parents, our communities, our causes. Let's start doing it with more intention and by using the financial resources at our disposal in ways that are specific, smart, and forward thinking. Where our kids are concerned, this starts when they're young as we educate them on how to make the most of the financial resources they have, put more money in their hands as they age to train them to handle it, and—hopefully—set them on a course toward independence. With our parents, the challenge is helping in ways that make the most of their resources and, when contributing our own, doing it in a way that doesn't sabotage our own financial fortitude in later life. Finally, we can and should take all this financial power and use it to do good—good for our families, the causes we care about, and in a bigger way (by investing, giving, and spending thoughtfully) for the world.

I hope that you've enjoyed going on this journey with me. It's one I continue every week on the *HerMoney* podcast, in the private HerMoney Facebook group, and at HerMoney.com. Please join me there—and if you're so inclined, take a moment and drop me a note about your experience as a woman with money. I promise, I'll read them all.

Jean Chatzky
August 28, 2018

Acknowledgments

When it comes to books, it always feels a little unfair to me that the author's name goes front and center when, in reality, we know these are group projects—and this one is no exception. I am hugely indebted to the many people who helped bring *Women with Money* from conception to the page. The highly skilled Kate Ashford and Beth Braverman contributed fabulous and detailed additional reporting. My agent, Heather Jackson, helped fine-tune the pitch and guided me and the book all the way through to publication. I had the good fortune to work with two editorial teams at Grand Central and want to thank them all: Karen Murgolo, who acquired this book; Gretchen Young and Karen Kosztolnyik, who saw it through; and the wonderful Grand Central Team, including Morgan Hedden, Amanda Pritzker, Nick Small, Jarrod Taylor, and Mari Okuda, have provided me with a supportive, welcoming publishing home. Ashley Sandberg brought her wit and energy to helping this project find the limelight. Lindsay Walsh, Elaine Sherman, Kelly Hultgren, Lisa Greene, Kathryn Tuggle, Kathy Goldberg, and Eliot Kaplan read early chapters and drafts and helped me find my way. And many, many sources shared their knowledge and experience (you can see their names beginning on page 249). This book wouldn't exist without every one of them.

I'm also fortunate to have many wonderful people in my work life, supporting this project and others. At HerMoney.com: Kelly

Hultgren, David Wieder, Kathryn Tuggle, Hattie Burgher, Katie Doyle, and Sigward Moser. At the *HerMoney Podcast*: Charles DeMontebello and the team at CDM. At NBC: Libby Leist, Savannah Guthrie, Hoda Kotb, Tom Mazzarelli, Debbie Kosovsky, Minah Kathuria, Karen Trosset, Elena Nachmanoff, and Melea McCreary. At Fidelity: Alexandra Taussig, Jeanne Thompson, Lorna Kapusta, Weisia Sadowski, Melissa Tansey, Colleen Rolph, Kristen Robinson, Jaime Guild, and Kellie Carvalho. At PwC: Mitch Roschelle and Shannon Schuyler. At AARP: Tom Previ, Mary Liz Burns, Ali Goewey, George Mannes, Bob Love, and Karen Horrigan. At Jackson: Michael Falcon, Emilio Pardo, Cyrus Bamji, and Beth Larson. Thank you.

Finally, I want to thank my friends and family—the ones who keep me sane even when I'm in the depths of (as we call it) "book hell": Diane, Jan, Kathy, Debi, Ilene, Jodie, and Lisa; my kids, Jake, Julia, Emily, Sam, and Shelby (welcome to the family); my brothers, Eric and Dave, and my sister-in-law, Ali; my mom and stepdad, Elaine and Bob; and, of course, my husband Eliot, who makes life better every single day. I love you all.

Sources and Resources

I'm grateful to the many people who were generous with their time and expertise in the researching of this book. I've tried to credit them in the text, but also want you to be able to follow up and learn more from them on your own.

Individuals

Gina Aldaz, wealth management advisor, Talis Advisors, Plano, TX

Robin Arzon, vice president of Fitness Programming and head instructor, Peloton, and author of *Shut Up and Run*

Maggie Baker, PhD, psychologist, financial therapy specialist, and author of *Crazy About Money*

John Bodnar, CFP, founder/CEO of Bodnar Financial Advisors

Mika Brzezinski, cohost, *Morning Joe*, MSNBC, and author of *Know Your Value*

Nancy Butler, CFP, speaker and author of *Above All Else: Success in Life and Business*

Amy Castoro, president and CEO, the Williams Group, and coauthor of *Bridging Generations: Transitioning Family Wealth and Values for a Sustainable Legacy*

Lisa Chastain, money coach specializing in millennials and author of *Girl, Get Your Shit Together!: Control Your Money, Live Purposefully, and Love Your Life! #Adulting Your Way*

Amanda Clayman, financial therapist, Los Angeles

David Clingingsmith, associate professor of economics, Weatherhead School of Management, Case Western Reserve University, Cleveland, OH

Kathleen Cronin, regional outreach and communications coordinator, NJSBDC Bergen County (Small Business Development Center)

Vincent Cucuzza, CFP, Barnum Financial Group, Elmsford, NY

Eric J. Dammann, PhD, clinical psychologist/psychoanalyst and executive coach, New York, NY

William Davis, CFP, Ameriprise Financial, Yardley, PA

Nathan Dungan, founder of Share Save Spend, which helps individuals and families develop healthy money habits that honor their values and enhance their financial well-being

Dan Egan, director of behavioral finance and investing, Betterment

Joe Elsasser, CFP, creator of Social Security Timing software, and managing partner, Sequent Planning, Omaha

Dave Fanger, CEO, Swell Investing

Marlow and Chris Felton, financial advisors and authors of *Couples Money: What Every Couple Should Know About Money and Relationships*

Jane Wolf Frances, social worker, lawyer, psychotherapist, and author of *Parenting Our Parents*

Stacy Francis, president and CEO, Francis Financial, New York, NY

Amber Freeman, head of research, Swell Investing

Megan Gorman, managing partner, Chequers Financial Management, and writer, *The Wealth Intersection* (blog)

Lisa Gould, personal financial consultant and life coach

Michael Hackard, founder, Hackard Law, and author of *The Wolf at the Door: Undue Influence and Elder Financial Abuse*

Linda Henman, "the Decision Catalyst," author of *Tough Calls: How to Move Beyond Indecision and Good Intentions*

Mindy Jensen, community manager of BiggerPockets, author of *How to Sell Your Home: The Essential Guide to a Fast, Stress-Free, and Profitable Sale*, and cohost of *BiggerPockets Money Podcast*

Alexander Joyce, retirement planner and president/CEO, ReJoyce Financial, Carmel, IN

Eliot Kaplan, career coach, Westchester, NY, eliotkaplancoaching.com

Michael Kay, CFP, Livingston, NJ, author of *The Feel Rich Project: Reinventing Your Understanding of True Wealth to Find True Happiness*

Brad Klontz, PsyD, CFP, founder, Financial Psychology Institute, associate professor of practice in financial psychology, Creighton University Heider College of Business, and author of *Mind over Money: Overcoming the Money Disorders That Threaten Our Financial Health*

Les Kotzer, wills and estates lawyer, and author of *The Wills Lawyers: Their Stories of Money, Inheritance, Greed, Family, and Betrayal*

Abe Lee, real estate agent, broker, real estate educator, and developer, Honolulu, HI

Joy Loverde, eldercare industry consultant and author of *Who Will Take Care of Me When I'm Old?*

Christine Luken, "financial lifeguard," financial coach, and author of *Money Is Emotional: Prevent Your Heart from Hijacking Your Wallet*

Larry Mandelker, estate and trusts lawyer, Seyfarth Shaw, New York, NY

Elle Martinez, creator and host, Couple Money website and podcast, and author of *Jumpstart Your Marriage and Your Money: A 4-Week Guide to Building Wealth Together*

Shannon McCracken, chief development officer, Charity Navigator

Lance McHan, former real estate appraiser and investment property owner, and current real estate agent, Stockton, CA

Tracie McMillion, CFA, head of global asset allocation strategy, Wells Fargo Investment Institute

Ryan McPherson, CFP, Atlanta

Eric Meermann, CFP and EA, Palisades Hudson Financial Group

William Meyer, founder and managing principal, Social Security Solutions

Sarah Newcomb, senior behavioral scientist, Morningstar, and author of *Loaded: Money, Psychology, and How to Get Ahead Without Leaving Your Values Behind*

Cady North, CFP, CEO, and financial advisor, North Financial Advisors, Washington, DC

Michael Norton, professor of business administration, Harvard Business School; member, Behavioral Insights Group, Harvard; and coauthor of *Happy Money: The Science of Happier Spending*

Susan Oleari, Chicago regional president, Bank of Montreal

Una Osili, professor of economics and associate dean for research and international programs, Lilly Family School of Philanthropy, Indiana University

Kate Paine, owner, Standing Out Online, and former executive director, Women Business Owners Network, Vermont, 2010–2013

Scott and Bethany Palmer, a.k.a. "the Money Couple"

Lauren Papp, professor of human development and family studies, University of Wisconsin–Madison

Fran Pastore, founder, president, and CEO, Women's Business Development Council

Leisa Peterson, CFP, business strategist, money coach, and host of the podcast *Art of Abundance*

Deborah Price, founder, the Money Coaching Institute, and author of *The Heart of Money: A Couple's Guide to Creating True Financial Intimacy*

Marc Prosser, cofounder, FitSmallBusiness.com

Bruce Purdy, acting assistant administrator, Office of Women's Business Ownership, SBA

Cari Rauch, life and money coach

Victor Ricciardi, assistant professor of financial management and behavioral finance and risk expert, Goucher College

Ellen Rogin, CFP, Northfield, IL

Carolyn Rosenblatt, elder law attorney and mediator with a background in nursing; founder, AgingParents.com; and author of *The Family Guide to Aging Parents: Answers to Your Legal, Financial, and Healthcare Questions*

Belinda Rosenblum, CPA, financial strategist at OwnYourMoney.com

Gena Rotstein, philanthropic wealth advisor, Karma & Cents, social impact lab, Calgary

Gretchen Rubin, author of *The Happiness Project* and cohost of the podcast *Happier with Gretchen Rubin*

Mary Jo Saavedra, gerontologist, aging life care manager, and author of *Eldercare 101*

Carolyn Saunders, head of pensions and long-term savings, Pinsent Masons, London

Carrie Spaulding, career and relationship coach, the Thirtysomething Coach, carriespaulding.com

Barbara Stanny, speaker, money/wealth coach, and author of *Overcoming Undearning*, *Secrets of Six-Figure Women*, and *Prince Charming Isn't Coming*

Kristin Sullivan, CFP, Denver, CO

Denise Supplee, Realtor, property management specialist, real estate investment educator, operations director, and cofounder of SparkRental

Alexandra Taussig, senior vice president, women and investing, analytics, marketing & communications, Fidelity Investments

Jacquette Timmons, financial behaviorist, and president and CEO, Sterling Investment Management

Cindy Troianello, financial coach and author of *Money Smart Happy Heart: Have the Happiness Money Can't Buy and the Big Things It Can!*

Susan Turnbull, founder and principal, Personal Legacy Advisors, and author of *The Wealth of Your Life: A Step-by-Step Guide to Creating Your Ethical Will*

Mikelann R. Valterra, certified money coach and accredited financial counselor, and cofounder of MoneyMinderOnline.com

Laura Vanderkam, author of *I Know How She Does It: How Successful Women Make the Most of Their Time* and *All the Money in the World: What the Happiest People Know About Getting and Spending*

Sharon Vornholt, real estate investor and author of *Louisville Gals Real Estate Blog* (LouisvilleGalsRealEstateBlog.com)

Patrick Wanis, PhD, human behavior and relationship expert, Miami, FL

Judith Ward, CFP, T. Rowe Price

Karen Southall Watts, "professional encourager," entrepreneurial coach, and author of *Ask and Achieve: Questions in the Middle of a Woman's Life*

Tensie Whelan, director, NYU Center for Sustainable Business, and clinical professor, business and society

Nicole Wipp, elder law/estate planning principal attorney and founder, Family & Aging Law Center, Milford, MI

Studies

Fewer women ask for business financing (Fundera, May 2017), https://www.fundera.com/blog/the-state-of-online-small-business-lending-q2-2016

Opportunity versus Necessity Entrepreneurship: Two Components of Business Creation, https://siepr.stanford.edu/sites/default/files/publications/17-014.pdf

Women business owners and borrowing: https://bschool.pepperdine.edu/news/2017/11/women-business-owners-struggle-get-business-loans-inc/

Raising Kids Who Launch: https://www.fidelity.com/bin-public/060_www_fidelity_com/documents/Family-Finance-Study-Executive-Summary.pdf

"Women Feel Less Safe Than Men in Many Developed Countries," Gallup, http://news.gallup.com/poll/155402/women-feel-less-safe-men-developed-countries.aspx

"Sex Differences in Physician Salary in US Public Medical Schools," *JAMA*, https://jamanetwork.com/journals/jamainternalmedicine/fullarticle/2532788

"Women and Money in Australia: Across the Generations," Rozlin Russell, Jozica Kutin, Rachael Green, Marcus Banks, Amalia Di Iorio, RMIT University, 2016

The Allianz Women, Money, and Power Study, Allianz Life, https://www.allianzlife.com/about/news-and-events/news-releases/Women-Money-and-Power-Study

"Are Women More Emotional Than Men?," *Psychology Today*, www
.psychologytoday.com/blog/sexual-personalities/201504/are
-women-more-emotional-men

Sharing Bank Accounts, Bankrate: http://www.bankrate.com/personal
-finance/credit/money-pulse-0517/

Financial Infidelity, CreditCards.com: https://www.creditcards.com/credit
-card-news/financial-infidelity-cheating-poll.php

Retirement Smile Curve, Morningstar: https://corporate.morningstar
.com/ib/documents/MethodologyDocuments/ResearchPapers
/Blanchett_True-Cost-of-Retirement.pdf

Long-Term Health Care Costs, Fidelity: https://www.fidelity.com/view
points/retirement/retiree-health-costs-rise

Consumer Spending, Bank of America: https://promo.bankofamerica
.com/friendsagain/assets/images/BOA_2017-Trends-in-Consumer
-Mobility-Report_Wave3-V7.pdf

Women and Money, Fidelity: https://www.fidelity.com/bin-public/060
_www_fidelity_com/documents/women-fit-money-study.pdf

Long-Term Care Insurance Costs, American Association for Long-
Term Care Insurance: http://www.aaltci.org/news/long-term-care
-insurance-association-news/long-term-care-insurance-prices
-drop-aaltcis-2018-price-index-reports

Finland/UK Study on Social Groups: https://www.ncbi.nlm.nih.gov
/pmc/articles/PMC4852646/

Keeping Up with the Joneses, Morningstar: http://www.morningstar
.com/lp/the-comparison-trap

Value of an Advisor, Morningstar: https://corporate1.morningstar.com
/uploadedFiles/US/AlphaBetaandNowGamma.pdf

Value of an Advisor, Envestnet: http://www.envestnet.com/content
/docs/capital-sigma-sources-advisor-created-value

Value of an Advisor, Vanguard: https://advisors.vanguard.com/iwe
/pdf/FASQAAAB.pdf

Women-Owned Businesses, American Express: https://www.american
express.com/us/small-business/openforum/articles/women

-owned-firms-springing/?linknav=us-of-keywords-findmore
-findmore-stateofwomen-ownedbusinessesreport-article

David Clingingsmith Research: http://faculty.weatherhead.case.edu
/clingingsmith/NEIW.pdf

Daniel Kahneman Research: http://www.pnas.org/content/107/38/16489
.full

The Emotional Impact of Having Money in the Bank: https://www
.ncbi.nlm.nih.gov/pubmed/27064287

Michael Norton on Prosocial Spending: https://happylabubc.files.word
press.com/2014/02/dunn-aknin-norton_prosocial_cdips.pdf

Couples and Money, *Money* magazine: http://time.com/money/2800576
/love-money-by-the-numbers/

Mom Spending Guilt, BabyCenter: https://www.babycenter.com/0_moms
-and-money-how-to-beat-spending-guilt-financial-stress-a
_2422237.bc

Stressful Life Events, Fidelity and Stanford University: https://www
.businesswire.com/news/home/20170502005877/en/Life-Happens
.-Health-Wealth-Connected-Fidelity-Research

Eldercare Conversations, Fidelity: https://www.fidelity.com/bin-public
/060_www_fidelity_com/documents/Family-Finance-Study
-Executive-Summary.pdf

Cost of Care, Genworth: https://www.genworth.com/about-us/industry
-expertise/cost-of-care.html

Emotional Stress of Caregivers: http://www.prweb.com/releases/2015/06
/prweb12765231.htm

Cost of Informal Caregiving: https://www.rand.org/news/press/2014/10
/27.html

Lost Wages, Met Life: https://www.aarp.org/content/dam/aarp/livable
-communities/learn/health/metlife-study-of-caregiving-costs-to
-working-caregivers-2011-aarp.pdf

Cognitive Impairment: https://academic.oup.com/psychsocgerontology
/article/58/3/S179/583380

"Housing America's Older Adults," Harvard, http://www.jchs.harvard
.edu/research/housing_americas_older_adults

Long-Term Care Expectations, Age Wave: https://mlaem.fs.ml.com
/content/dam/ML/Articles/pdf/ML_Finance-Study-Report
_2017.pdf

Estate Plans, LexisNexis: https://www.lexisnexis.com/en-us/about-us
/media/press-release.page?id=1311095221427043

Having a Will, Caring.com: https://www.caring.com/articles/wills-survey
-2017

"Gender Differences in Giving," *ScienceDaily*: https://www.sciencedaily
.com/releases/2017/10/171009123213.htm

"Waiting for Merlot: Anticipatory Consumption of Experiential and
Material Purchases," *Psychological Science*, October 2014

"How Your Bank Balance Buys Happiness: The Importance of 'Cash on
Hand' to Life Satisfaction," *Emotion*, August 2016

"Buying Time Promotes Happiness," *Proceedings of the National Academy of Sciences of the United States of America*, July 2017

"Prosocial Spending and Happiness: Using Money to Benefit Others Pays Off," *Current Directions in Psychological Science*, February 2014

A Few of My Favorite Resources

Find a financial therapist: https://www.financialtherapyassociation.org/

Find a lawyer for a prenup: http://aaml.org/

Check your Social Security statement: SSA.gov

Determine a Social Security strategy: SocialSecuritySolutions.com or
MaximizeMySocialSecurity.com

Choose a financial planner: Garrett Planning Network, NAPFA.org,
XY PlanningNetwork, FPANet.org

Background check an advisor: BrokerCheck.org, PaladinRegistry.com,
BBB.org

Calculate your long-term care insurance costs: https://www.genworth
.com/long-term-care-insurance/source/make-a-plan/ltc-insurance
-cost.html

Keep a time log: http://lauravanderkam.com/books/168-hours/manage
-your-time/

Care for an older parent: AARP.org/caregiving (also in Spanish), Eldercare .gov, Caregiver.org, benefitscheckup.org

Find a geriatric care manager: Aginglifecare.org

Create a basic will: LegalZoom.com

Find an estate planning attorney: LegalMatch.com

Vet a charity: CharityNavigator.org, Guidestar.org, BBB.org

Create an ethical will: http://www.personallegacyadvisors.com/store /the-wealth-of-your-life/

Index

Jean Chatzky is the longtime financial editor of NBC's *Today* show, an award-winning personal finance journalist, and CEO of HerMoney .com, a multimedia company changing the relationships women have with money, inspired by her weekly podcast *HerMoney with Jean Chatzky*. Jean also proudly serves as the financial ambassador for AARP and writes a column for *AARP The Magazine*. Her most recent book, *AgeProof: Living Longer Without Running Out of Money or Breaking a Hip*, coauthored with Dr. Michael Roizen, was a *New York Times* and *Wall Street Journal* best-seller. In 2015, Jean teamed up with the PwC Charitable Foundation and *Time for Kids* to launch *Your $*, an in-school personal finance magazine reaching more than two million fourth, fifth, and sixth graders each month. Although she'll always be a Midwesterner at heart, Jean lives with her family in Westchester County, NY.

For details about how to hold your own HerMoney Happy Hour and more resources, go to: www.WomenWithMoneyBook.com.